D0800702

CHILDREN OF DIVORCE
Stories of Loss and Growth

CHILDREN OF DIVORCE

Stories of Loss and Growth

John H. Harvey
University of Iowa

Mark A. Fine
University of Missouri

LEA

LAWRENCE ERLBAUM ASSOCIATES, PUBLISHERS
2004   Mahwah, New Jersey   London

Lawrence Erlbaum Associates, Inc., Publishers
10 Industrial Avenue
Mahwah, New Jersey 07430

Cover design by Kathryn Houghtaling Lacey

Library of Congress Cataloging-in-Publication Data

Harvey, John H., 1943–
    Children of divorce : stories of loss and growth / John H. Harvey,
    Mark A. Fine.
        p.   cm.
Includes bibliographical references and index.
ISBN 0-8058-4668-9 (cloth : alk. paper)
ISBN 0-8058-4669-7 (pbk. : alk. paper)
1. Children of divorced parents—United States—Case studies.
    2. Divorce—United States—Case studies. 3. Parent and child—
    United States—Case studies.   I. Fine, Mark A.   II. Title.
HQ777.5H38   2004
306.89'0973—dc22   2003060385
                                                              CIP

Books published by Lawrence Erlbaum Associates are printed on
acid-free paper, and their bindings are chosen for strength and
durability.

Printed in the United States of America
10   9   8   7   6   5   4   3   2

This book is dedicated to the hundreds of students who contributed their stories to the development of this book.

*It is their voice, reflecting vividly
their experiences of loss and growth,
that makes this book and its information valuable
to all people who care about the effects of divorce.*

CONTENTS

PREFACE

At this point in my life, I'm almost positive that I'll never get married. There's a 0.5% chance of my getting married. I'm just so disillusioned by the whole concept. I don't think my parents divorce has affected me negatively that much. Their marriage, however, has screwed me up more than I'll probably ever know.

—A 20-year-old child of divorce

It was commentaries such as the one above that originally stimulated this project for John H. Harvey. The commentaries were collected in his classes over a period of approximately 6–7 years (see chap. 2 for a discussion of the method). These words of anguish, which frequently were offset by words of relief and hope, suggested the value of allowing students whose parents have divorced to provide narratives to assist all of us in better understanding the depth and breadth of their experience. Harvey was privileged to have Mark A. Fine come on board later to provide his own perspective based on research and teaching in the field of relationship dissolution and divorce for many years. The book then became a true collaboration between them and the many students who contributed narratives for this book. This book was written for scholars, practitioners, educators, and the educated public. It is meant to represent some of the diversity of voices about divorce in the 21st century. As we describe in the opening chapters, divorce is taking a toll on our society. It also is leading some young people to develop into mature, empathic persons well beyond their time. We hope that people in general will be educated by the stories told by young people in these pages.

We wrote this book because the loss of our close, intimate relationships is an often devastating experience that each one of us will experience in life. Divorce and dissolution have been occurring at an exceedingly high rate for the last 30 years in the United States. Most people in this country have been affected at least indirectly by cultural changes attributable to divorce.

We wrote the book from personal experience in losing many relationships to breakup, including divorce, and as college professors and researchers in the field of close relationships. As professors, we have heard many stories of relationship loss.

In this book, we report and comment on a selected set of scholars' arguments about divorce. Then, the stories of young people directly affected by divorce in their families form the core of this book. These stories have been collected mainly from hundreds of Harvey's students in the last few years and are reported with the students' permission. The students' commentaries are presented in italics.

This book paints a picture both of the *pain* and the *hope* shown by people in the throes of divorce and dissolution, during the period of dissolution and for years later. We believe that if we can learn from the pain of dissolution, we are making progress in recognizing the long-term widespread impacts of divorce. This book also is very much about hope and the will to survive developed in adverse circumstances. We have attempted to report narratives that are balanced in showing hope and pain, often in the same person.

This book challenges the contention that most children of divorce will be irretrievably hurt by their parents' divorce. It presents a mixture of young people's voices, showing the great variety of reactions to parental divorce. It shows the strength and resilience many of these young people have learned in surviving the pain and confusion surrounding divorce in their families. The book emphasizes how hope about the possibilities and merits of having close relationships, and the willingness to try to have stronger families in their own adult lives, represent abiding motivations in this sample of young persons.

As will be described in chapters 1 and 2, we provide an overarching theoretical emphasis on the value of storytelling for people dealing with major losses. The stories presented are often raw and visceral in tone and content. It is our hope that this method of stressing the raw input of respondents will make the experiences more vivid and realistic to the reader. Our overall goal with this approach is to enhance both an understanding of and compassion for children of divorce and for the parents who strive to make the child's welfare the highest priority in their postdivorce lives.

ACKNOWLEDGMENTS

We wish to thank Debra Riegert, Senior Editor at Lawrence Erlbaum Associates, Inc., for suggesting our collaboration on this book and for many helpful inputs to our work. We also thank reviewers of drafts of the book, including David H. Demo, Lawrence H. Ganong, and Terri L. Orbuch. We thank Jason Planer and Sarah Wahlert of Lawrence Erlbaum Associates, Inc., for their helpful work on this project. We thank the significant others in our lives for their contributions to our lives during the time of our work on this book, including Patrick and Barbara for John H. Harvey and Loreen, Aubrey, Julia, Aristotle, and Kennedy for Mark A. Fine. Finally, as we note in the Dedication, our gratitude is extended to the hundreds of students who believed enough in the value of storytelling to communicate their stories for this project.

—*John H. Harvey*
—*Mark A. Fine*
Fall 2003

1

A CULTURE OF DIVORCE
AND THE VALUE OF DIVERSE VOICES

WHY THIS BOOK?

Why are we (John Harvey and Mark Fine) writing this book? We are writing it because the loss of one's close, intimate relationships is a daunting, sometimes devastating experience that each one of us will experience in life. It also has been occurring at a contagious rate for the last 30 years in U.S. society and now stretches to most parts of the Western world. All of us will experience such losses in the form of breakups of romantic relations, and millions of us will be directly affected by divorce in our lives. All of us will be affected at least indirectly by cultural changes attributable to divorce (e.g., see later discussion about the increased role of grandparents in taking on primary parenting duties in the 21st century).

We also write both from personal experience in losing many relationships to breakups, including divorce, and from the standpoint of being college professors and researchers in the field of close relationships. In this latter role, we have heard countless stories of relationship loss. Indeed, the core of this book is about discourses of divorce. First, we will report and comment on a selected set of scholars' arguments about divorce in the 21st century. Then we present the stories of many young people directly affected by divorce in their families; these stories will form the centerpiece of this book. They have been collected from hundreds of John Harvey's students in the last few years and are reported with the students' permission; names and various specific details have been changed as necessary to ensure anonymity.

The pain associated with the loss of close relationships is a cultural burden of vast proportions. It extends beyond the persons who dissolve their relationships to children, parents, and dear friends. We also write as parents who are trying to help their own children (Harvey: a young son; Fine: two teenage daughters) deal with—and, we hope even thrive in the context of—their parents' divorce. This extremely important topic receives considerable attention in this book. Many scholars and writers are weighing in on the impacts of divorce on children. We do, too, from the vantage point of personal accounts by children and a review of the best evidence that exists on this topic.

What we hope to represent best in this book are both the *pain* and the *hope* shown by people in the throes of divorce and marital dissolution, during the dissolution and for years later. We try to represent this *pain* with the accounts of many young people. We believe that if we can learn from this pain, we are making progress in recognizing the long-term widespread impacts of divorce. We can make relationships better. We must work very hard to make them better, because the alternative, as documented here, is often devastating to all who are enduring this pain.

This book is as much about *hope*, strength gained from coping with loss, resolve to live life honestly and with breadth of understanding as it is about dismay, pain, and hopelessness. The narratives that are reported are balanced in showing hope and pain, often in the same person. These stories tell of how valiantly people struggle to cope in the midst of great interpersonal storms. And they sometimes are successful. Such stories may serve as models for others facing similar dilemmas.

A DIVORCING CULTURE

The great increase in the divorce rate, from 3 out of 10 marriages ending in divorce in 1960 to 5 out of 10 by 1975, and a continued high rate into the 21st century, has had many untoward effects on society (Whitehead, 1996). Economically speaking, marital dissolution is hard on all parties, especially on women (Hetherington & Kelly, 2002; McLanahan, 1999). Compared with children whose parents remain married, children of divorced parents also experience higher rates of a number of different problems, such as internalizing behaviors (e.g., anxiety, depression), externalizing problems (e.g., behavior problems), and poor school performance (in particular, dropping out of school; Emery, 1999; Fine, 2000; Fine et al., 1999), although, as we note in more detail later in this book, the differences between groups tend to be relatively small, with considerable variability within each group.

Although it is obvious that marital dissolution affects the individual members of divorced families, the implications of the rapid rise in the divorce rate up until around 1980 (after which the divorce rate has remained quite stable) extend beyond the single-family unit to affect such areas as government policy, provision of mental health services, and society as a whole. In this context of relatively high divorce rates, federal policy has been drafted to attempt to improve child support compliance rates and to address a number of other political issues relevant to the family (Bogenschneider, 2000). In addition, in the last 20 years there has been a tremendous increase in the number of mental health professionals working on relationships and divorce issues, to the point where divorce-related intervention programs, such as mediation and parent education programs for divorcing parents, have become increasingly popular and often mandated (Feng & Fine, 2000). Parent education programs for divorcing parents, in particular, have clearly become "big business" (Feng & Fine, 2000).

EFFECTS OF DIVORCE ON CHILDREN

The topic of divorce and children is in the news regularly and has received much attention in the last 20 years. At holiday times, children may experience some of their greatest feelings of loss because of split families, continued conflict between ex-partners, and the children's own divided loyalties. Special consideration of children's needs during these times is an important obligation for divorced parents. As one counselor told the *Chicago Tribune* (story by A. Levine, December 24, 2000, p. C2): "I'm preaching the same sermon I was 20 years ago ... and I am still astonished that people don't get it ... Before you do anything for Christmas, you need to get in your child's skin and then make a plan. Because what you do now is going to forever influence the way they look at the holidays."

The effects of divorce on children is a prime, timely topic, because in the early 21st century, data from the U.S. Bureau of the Census indicated that at least 50% to 60% of the children in the United States will spend some period of time before they reach age 18 in a home in which divorce has occurred, and one third or more of the children in the United States will live in a stepfamily by the time they reach age 18. Parental divorce is strongly statistically associated with adult children's divorces (Amato & Booth, 1997), a phenomenon commonly known as *intergenerational transmission of divorce.* Amato and Deboer (2001) found that parental divorce approximately doubled the chances that offspring would themselves divorce as adults.

There is an abundance of literature on the intergenerational transmission of divorce. Factors such as education, income, family and social support systems, and individual attitudes and expectations have been implicated as explaining why offspring of divorced parents are themselves more likely to divorce as adults (Feng, Giarrusso, Bengtson, & Frye, 1999). For example, compared with children from first-married families, children of divorced parents have been found to have lower income and educational attainment, to marry at younger ages, and to be more likely to cohabit prior to marriage (Furstenberg & Teitler, 1994). Amato and Deboer (2001) concluded that children from divorced families have a higher likelihood of themselves divorcing because they hold a "comparatively weak commitment to the norm of lifelong marriage" (p. 1038).

The types of reported negative effects of divorce on children are diverse and numerous. An August 1999 news story suggested that teen boys who have had limited or negative interaction histories with their fathers, often in connection with divorce, are at higher risk for smoking, drinking, and illegal drug usage than are teen boys with strong relationships with a single mother. As college teachers, we have seen and heard about the impacts of divorce on college students for more than 30 years. College students frequently report having been placed in the middle of interparental conflict, bitter struggles regarding money, new dating partners, wrongs such as infidelities at the time of their parents' breakups, and the like.

A number of popular books on divorce have recently been published by well-known scholars such as Wallerstein, Lewis, and Blakeslee (2000b) and Hetherington and Kelly (2002). These books have provided data and perspective on the effects of divorce on children and adults. These books are different from the previous writings by these (and other) authors because they are intended for a broader, nonacademic audience. Also, as we note later, because Hetherington and Wallerstein have quite different views on the effects of divorce on children, their divergent views received considerable national attention in such magazines as *Newsweek* and *Time*. The Hetherington–Wallerstein "debate" highlights a frustrating aspect of the divorce literature: Scholars often reach conflicting conclusions regarding how harmful divorce can be on children. For example, Hetherington and Kelly found that although there was initial turmoil in the lives of the children, their lives had become more normal by the second year after divorce and that there were few substantial long-term differences between these children and their counterparts from first-marriage families. By contrast, Wallerstein et al. (2000b) concluded that as many as one half of the young men and women they studied entered adulthood as worried, underachieving, self-deprecating, and sometimes angry people because of their parents' divorces. In an attempt to understand why scholars often reach different conclusions regarding the effects of divorce on family members, Fine and Demo (2000) argued that researchers' different theoretical perspectives, differing values, different disciplines, and differing training often leads them in divergent research directions and ultimately leads to the generation of different conclusions, sometimes even from the very same data.

A DIFFERENT APPROACH TO THE CONTROVERSY
REGARDING THE EFFECTS OF DIVORCE ON CHILDREN

How can one make sense of these very different threads in the literature—with some investigators emphasizing long-term pain and sadness and others emphasizing resilience and strength? A synthesis of
the literature by Emery (1999) may be helpful in making sense of
these apparently disparate conclusions. Emery proposed five "facts"
related to how divorce affects children: a) divorce causes a great
deal of stress for children; b) divorce increases the risk (often doubling it, depending on the dimension studied) of psychological
problems; c) despite the increased risk, most children from divorced families function as well as children from first-marriage families; d) children whose parents divorce report considerable pain,
unhappy memories, and continued distress; and e) individual differences in children's postdivorce adjustment are influenced by aspects of postdivorce family life, particularly the quality of the child's
relationship with the residential parent, the nature of interparental
conflict, the family's financial standing, and the nature of the relationship between the child and the nonresidential parent. According to Emery, some investigators, particularly Wallerstein, focus on
the fourth point without adequately considering the others,
whereas others tend to minimize the stress and pain experienced by
these children and young adults. In a sense, some scholars are
blinded in that they look only at one or two sides of the proverbial
multisided elephant. In this book we attempt to gain a more com-
prehensive view of the divorce elephant by emphasizing both the
pain and the resilience in students' stories and memories. In many
ways, the themes in this book are very much consistent with Emery's
analysis, in that we report on numerous aspects of the divorce process and experience, including pain and loss, as well as strength and
resilience. Next, we review some of the more important programs of
research, and the astute reader will note that there is differential
emphasis on the five "facts" Emery identified.

THE UNEXPECTED LEGACY OF DIVORCE

Wallerstein and Lewis (1998) reported on a 25-year follow-up longitudinal study of children and adolescents whose families had

separated and divorced. The respondents were followed with regular interviews beginning with the decisive separation. Wallerstein
and Lewis reported on the youngest respondents in the study (now
in their late 20s and early 30s). They found that the respondents'
earliest memories when the divorces were occurring were abandonment, terror, and loneliness. Adolescence was marked by early
sexual activity and experimentation with drugs or alcohol. The respondents' early adulthood also was marked by fewer resources for
college funding; fears of intimacy; and strained relationships with
their parents, particularly their fathers.

Wallerstein et al.'s (2000b) analysis of the effects of divorce on
children created quite a media frenzy. In their book, *The Unexpected Legacy of Divorce*, they reported on their 30 years of research
with children whose parents were divorcing in the 1970s. For these
131 children of 80 California families—a small and not-so-random
sample of the 1 million children whose parents divorce each
year—the data showed tremendous flux in their relationship lives
over the years after their parents divorced. Wallerstein et al. indicated that these individuals whose parents divorced spent much of
their early adulthood negotiating relationships. Many were not
married or interested in becoming married. Many did not want
children. More than one half of the respondents in the di-
vorced-family group had decided at that point in their lives to not
have children *for fear of condemning them to the same difficult childhood
they had experienced.* Wallerstein et al. (2000b) reported that many
of their respondents were intensely afraid of being abandoned—
more so than adults whose parents had not divorced.

Wallerstein et al. (2000b) found that 40% of adult children of divorce in their sample never married, compared with 24% in the
comparison group. About 40% of the marriages of the di-
vorced-family children ended in divorce, whereas only 9% of the
children from first-marriage families divorced. However, national
data indicate that about 35% of people from intact families divorce (Amato & Booth, 1997). It is unclear why there was so little
divorce, relatively speaking, in the children from intact families in
Wallerstein et al.'s work.

In Wallerstein et al.'s (2000b) study, children from families in
which the parents had reasonably good marriages, or even moder-
ately unhappy marriages, fared far better on most adjustment di-
mensions than did the children whose parents divorced. They

seemed to have a much better idea of what they wanted in a spouse, along with more stability in their close relationships and more clarity regarding the type of family they themselves wished to create. They also seemed to have memories of good models of marriage. They recalled readily how their parents had struggled and overcome differences and how they cooperated in crises. These models in turn provided guidelines and reassurance for them as they undertook marriage and parenthood.

Some of the common characteristics of adult children of divorce reported by Wallerstein et al. (2000b) are listed in Table 1.1.

The Lightning-Rod Term "Good-Enough" Marriage

Wallerstein et al. (2000b) proposed a most controversial idea: "The myth that if the parents have a poor marriage the children are going to be unhappy is not true" (p. 23). They argued further that children do not care if parents sleep in separate beds if the

TABLE 1.1

Characteristics of Adult Children of Divorce
(Based on Findings From Wallerstein et al., 2000)

- Sixty percent of children of divorce have trouble with social relationships.
- On average, they expect failure in their lives.
- In general, they have a strong fear of change, resulting from the feeling that their parents' divorce was not for the best.
- They tend to fear betrayal.
- They are likely to fear being alone.
- Although wary of commitment and falling in love, they value love, marriage, and parenthood.
- They tend to be remarkably compassionate and attuned to others' feelings.
- They are likely to be very close to their siblings.
- On average, they have trouble with substance abuse, and start at an earlier age than other children.
- They tend to have more difficulty in college and receive less encouragement from their parents to seek higher education.
- Fewer of them marry or have children; they tend to marry at younger ages and be more prone to divorce.

household runs well and if the parenting holds up. A "good-enough" marriage without violence or martyrdom or severe mental disorder will do for the children; that is, the children from such marriages will progress through their own adult relationships with much less turmoil than will children from even happily divorced families. According to Wallerstein et al., the divorce may, paradoxically, be the *solution* for the parents' problems and the *cause* of the children's problems.

Wallerstein et al. (2000b) argued that, although people who cannot stand one another any longer cannot be expected to stay together, spouses nevertheless should fully consider the impact of the split on the family before the breach is introduced to the children. They believe that, over time, the biggest costs of the divorce will be paid by the children. Wallerstein has said in interviews about this work that she is not against divorce per se but that more couples in our time should consider sticking it out—even if they are beset by infidelity, depression, sexual boredom, loneliness, rejection, and the like. This is a tall order for our time!

Critique

Of course, Wallerstein et al.'s (2000b) evidence and the related conclusions have stirred the passions of many critics. In general, their various writings from this long-term study have been criticized for relying on a relatively small, selective sample. From the original 131 children who began the study in 1971, only 93 were interviewed for the follow-up work reported in *The Unexpected Legacy of Divorce* (Wallerstein et al., 2000b). Furthermore, the sample of children whose parents divorced was not matched against a randomly sampled control group of children from first-marriage families; rather, the comparison sample of 44 young adults was recruited mainly from alumni networks at the high schools attended by respondents in the divorce group. This approach, although not as rigorous as one might like, still involves a valuable comparison—in an area of work in which the collection of longitudinal information requires highly diligent work by the investigators to track down respondents over time.

In the popular media, various critiques of Wallerstein et al.'s (2000b) data and conclusions have been registered. Writing in *Time*, Kathy Pollitt, author and columnist for the *Nation*, argued:

America doesn't need more "good enough" marriages full of depressed and bitter people. Nor does it need more pundits blaming women for destroying "the family" with what are, after all, reasonable demands for equality and self-development We need to acknowledge that there are lots of different ways to raise competent and well-adjusted children, which—as, according to virtually every family researcher who has worked with larger and more representative samples than Wallerstein's tiny handful—the vast majority of kids of divorce turn out to be. We've learned a lot about how to divorce since 1971. When Mom has enough money and Dad stays connected, when parents stay civil and don't bad mouth each other, kids do all right. The "good enough" divorce— why isn't that ever the cover story? (Pollitt, 2000)

Braver, who wrote *Divorced Dads: Shattering The Myths* (1998), criticized Wallerstein et al. (2000) for not acknowledging that there are many better designed, ongoing studies regarding the lives of children of divorce (Associated Press article, "The Legacy of Divorce?," *Dallas News,* January 14, 2001, p. D1). He also noted that the differences between the divorced and comparison groups in Wallerstein et al.'s (2000b) samples were quite small. In this same article, Joan Kelly—a former colleague of Wallerstein's (Wallerstein & Kelly, 1980)—was quoted as saying that she has misgivings about the emphasis on the negative in the Wallerstein et al. (2000b) conclusions. How much pathology in the lives of these children of divorce can be attributed to their parents' divorces versus the attitudes, values, beliefs, and actions of the children themselves? Critics, including Braver and Kelly, have suggested that the available data, from other researchers as well as Wallerstein, do not justify the causal inference that divorce is responsible for negative child outcomes. In addition, both Braver and Kelly were concerned about what they perceived to be Wallerstein et al.'s (2000b) rather jaundiced views about men's ability to be good husbands and fathers. They suggested that Wallerstein et al. (2000b) were taking the position that fathers are less essential in the parenting process than are mothers (a position that also has been argued among many psychologists over the last decade).

Scholars such as Furstenberg, Cherlin, and Emery have suggested that stronger evidence exists to support the view that the long-term harmful effects of divorce occur only for a minority of the children involved. They have admitted that many young adults likely retain painful memories of their parents' divorce. It does not follow, however, that these memories will impair these adult children's marriages or lives in general. Such theorists have argued that, if these children's parents had not divorced, they might have retained equally painful memories of their parents' conflict-ridden marriages. Furstenberg and Cherlin (1991) proposed that, whenever there is trouble in a marriage, children will suffer and that it is not particularly helpful for parents to stay together in order to alleviate their children's suffering. They found that children who live with two parents who persistently quarrel over important areas of family life show higher levels of distress and behavior problems than do children whose parents have divorced.

Beyond this point about conflicted relationships, there is evidence that, compared with their peers from first-marriage families, *some* children show enhanced levels of functioning in areas such as maturity, self-esteem, and empathy following divorce (Gately & Schwebel, 1992; Coleman, Ganong, & Fine, 2000). Why do some children blossom in these ways after their parents have divorced? Divorce may place responsibilities on the children (e.g., caretaking of younger siblings) that they are experienced enough and otherwise ready to handle. Success in managing these responsibilities, in turn, may enhance their self-esteem, as well as sensitivity to others' problems. Furthermore, children who learn that they can rise to the occasion during the adversity of divorce may develop a sense of strength and courage that will assist them when they encounter problems later in life.

"FOR BETTER OR FOR WORSE": HETHERINGTON'S ANALYSIS

Mavis Hetherington and John Kelly (2002) recently wrote a book for the general population that summarizes results from Hetherington's extensive programmatic line of research into divorce, involving almost 1,400 families and 2,500 children from three major longitudinal studies. Hetherington and Kelly argued that society's view of divorce is "unremittingly negative" because of a variety of methodological limitations in previous studies, including that they have examined only individuals for a short time after the divorce and that they have not made use of a comparison group of individuals and families who have not experienced divorce. By contrast, Hetherington and Kelly claimed that their view is both novel and more balanced because of the comprehensiveness and depth of the research.

As Hetherington stated:

> *After forty years of research, I harbor no doubts about the ability of divorce to devastate. It can and does ruin lives. I've seen it happen more times than I like to think about. But that said, I also think much current writing on divorce—both popular and academic—has exaggerated its negative effects and ignored its sometimes considerable positive effects. Divorce has undoubtedly rescued many adults and children from the horror of domestic abuse, but it is not just a preventative measure. I have seen divorce provide many women and girls, in particular, with a remarkable opportunity for life-transforming personal growth. (p. 5)*

Another novel aspect of Hetherington and Kelly's (2002) book is the explicit acknowledgement of the diversity of postdivorce experiences that family members experience in today's society. According to Hetherington, the "divorce revolution" of the 1960s led not only to numerous changes in patterns of intimate relationships, including greater instability, but also to a wider range of life choices and options. Hetherington and Kelly argued that family life in America, and postdivorce family life in particular, has become more complex and diverse in the last 40 years. In turn, this greater complexity and diversity belie attempts to make overly simplistic inferences, such as "divorce is harmful to children" or "divorce has few long-term negative effects." In the narratives in subsequent chapters of this book, we see numerous examples of family circumstances that demonstrate the complex and contextualized nature of adjustment to divorce.

THE LOVE THEY LOST

In a book titled *The Love They Lost*, Staal (2000) argued that divorce has permeated all aspects of U.S. society in the 21st century. She reported on the experiences of 120 adult children of divorce, from people in their 20s to those in their 40s, whom she interviewed. Staal begins her analysis by describing her own parents' divorce when she was 13:

*Like most children of divorce, I spent much of my adolescence
caught up in dealing with the day-to-day negotiating myself
between two parents who were not especially fond of each other.
I blindly steered my way through what has now become
familiar territory, the landscape of single parenthood and
divided loyalties so carefully mapped out in the public
consciousness. What I didn't realize until I left home was
that, in the process, I had built my own emotional topography,
one that could not be left behind, no matter how far I tried to
run away from the past. (p. 2)*

An important point in Staal's (2000) argument is that the impacts are not just on children whose parents divorced, but on all the people in society. This point is reinforced in chapter 6 of this book in which young people report not only on the chaos in the lives of their family of origin but also in other families whom they have known well. Staal argued that the divorce culture is characterized by uncertainty and increasing numbers of couples living together before getting married (estimated to be 5.5 million in the United States in 2001) and waiting to get married—if they marry at all. She says that she, in her early 30s, represents America's first divorce generation, with divorce an omnipresent part of the generation's lives and a part of who they are: "Divorce plants a splinter in our minds, and, in response, we assemble our identities around it" (p. 9).

The essence of many of the commentaries Staal (2000) obtained from her respondents is that divorce has created a void in their lives. Although we found numerous stories of hope and resilience and present some of them in chapter 4 of this book, Staal reported few areas of growth and strength. She concluded from these commentaries that the respondents missed out too often on seeing a good model of a well-functioning couple. Such models are viewed as essential in order for the child to be able to effectively negotiate intimacy as an adult. One might wonder, though, what type of model would have been provided by married parents with poor-quality marriages.

Some of the many negative life themes reported by Staal's respondents and that are believed to be derived from their parents' divorce are listed in Table 1.2.

On the positive side, it was clear from Staal's (2000) respondents that many of them had become quite mature relatively early in life.

TABLE 1.2

Negative Impacts of Divorce on Adult Children of Divorce

- Fear of feeling, with emotional numbness lasting for many into adulthood, and with some lying when they suggested that the divorce only had positive effects for them.
- Fear of abandonment by loved ones caused by the actual events at the time of separation, when usually a parent left the home in some dramatically painful way.
- Confusion, fear, and anger because the divorce violated the children's expectations of family, with much blame and anger if one of the parents had an affair or did something that was considered highly disgraceful to the family.
- A feeling that many had to "kiss childhood good-bye" much too soon.
- Patterns of acting out against authority, getting in trouble at school and with the law, and problems in sexual relationships.
- Considerable emphasis on independence and self-sufficiency.
- Uncertainty about decisions in matters of love.
- Difficulty in coming to terms with both parents, especially a parent who may have been absent during the person's childhood and adolescence.

Note. Adapted from Staal (2000).

Their emphasis on personal autonomy and self-sufficiency was part of this maturity. Many also said that they had divorced but had learned how to "do" divorce civilly and with respect for children's needs and feelings because of their careful observation of unhelpful patterns that their parents displayed with them.

AMATO AND BOOTH'S (1997) WORK AND "A GENERATION AT RISK"

Amato and Booth, both sociologists, have produced, along with their colleagues, valuable evidence about children of divorce. For example, Amato and Keith (1991) found that in 97 studies involving 13,000 children ranging in age from preschool to young adulthood, children from divorced families were, *on average, somewhat worse off* than children who had lived in first-marriage families. These children of divorce had experienced more difficulty in school, more behavior problems, and more trouble getting along with their parents. Again, however, the differences between the groups were relatively small, which indicates that other factors besides divorce must have an influential role in determining children's adjustment. Some of the most important predictors of less positive child development include having an uninvolved or absent parent, economic deprivation and hardship, and stressful life changes. An important predictor of how well a person will adjust to divorce and the subsequent remarriage of his or her parents is how well the new stepfamily helps the person cope with stresses associated with the divorce (Coleman & Ganong, 1997; Lansford, Ceballo, Abbey, & Stewart, 2001). Although quite challenging, stepparents can learn to navigate ambiguous insider–outsider roles within their new family form. It may take time, but there are many good models in the huge population of blended families.

In a book titled *A Generation at Risk*, Amato and Booth (1997) presented results from a longitudinal study of 2,000 randomly chosen (which is a great strength, because it allows the researchers to make inferences about the general population) parents and offspring. The work was done over a period that ranged from 1980 to follow-up points in 1992 and 1995. Information from respondents came from telephone interviews. Parents' ages ranged from the late 30s to early 60s, and children's ages ranged from 19 to 40.

Amato and Booth (1997) found that *poor marriages* (defined by the participants as involving consistently high levels of conflict and distancing) harmed children in multiple ways. The children from these families, in which divorce had not yet occurred, showed problematic relations with parents. They also showed less affection, consensus, and perceived support; greater difficulty in dating (fewer dates, more problems); lower marital quality among married children; and relatively greater dissolution of close and married relationships among the offspring.

Children from divorced families showed similar patterns, *although they were not as pervasive as the effects of parents' low marital quality.* For example, they showed an increased probability of divorce, problems in interactions with their parents, lower education, lower occupational status, and greater economic adversity. There was some evidence of age effects, with younger children in general being more vulnerable both in divorce and low-marital quality settings. The link between parental marital quality and children's general well-being in adulthood was the most consistent finding to emerge from the research.

Across groups, Amato and Booth (1997) found that greater father involvement in child care results in stronger affection between adult children and their fathers as well as better integration in adulthood. They suggested that the Family Leave Act of 1993 was a positive step toward increasing workplace flexibility, therefore enhancing both parents' time and energy for parenting. They also suggested that, even in divorce, friendly parental relations are conducive to the child's well-being in adulthood.

In the context of covenant marriage legislation (which has passed in a few states, making divorce harder to get; see Hawkins, Nock, Wilson, Sanchez, & Wright, 2002) and other public policy actions aimed at strengthening marriage, Amato and Booth (1997) suggested that these steps likely will not be too effective in stifling the divorce rate. Legislation is unlikely to make unhappy couples want to stay together. Amato and Booth suggested that such couples likely will do whatever it takes (including making up stories about their partner's alleged infidelities or abuse) to get the divorce accomplished. Furthermore, preliminary evidence (Hawkins et al., 2002) suggests that very few couples (approximately 5%) take advantage of covenant marriage contracts when they have the opportunity to do so.

Booth and Amato (2001) expanded on their earlier work by emphasizing the role of parental marital quality as it affects children later in their lives. They presented evidence from their ongoing longitudinal study indicating that the dissolution of low-conflict marriages is associated with a wide range of negative offspring outcomes, including adversely affected intimate heterosexual relations, less social support from friends and relatives, and less positive general psychological well-being. On the other hand, divorce among high- conflict couples appeared to have a relatively benign effect on children. Booth and Amato theorized that escape from a high-conflict marriage benefits children because it removes them from an aversive, stressful home setting. However, a divorce that is not preceded by a prolonged period of overt discord may represent an unexpected, unwelcome, and uncontrollable event that children are likely to experience as quite stressful. Booth and Amato suggested that divorce under these circumstances represents a major change in what may otherwise have been a secure—and, from the child's perspective, seemingly well-functioning—family.

Booth and Amato (2001) concluded, though, that the stress generated by parents who are continuously fighting is likely to exceed the stress associated with coping with a household led by a single parent. They concluded at the end of their book that "In general, our results suggest that divorce may be beneficial or harmful to children, depending on whether it reduces or increases the amount of stress to which children are exposed" (p. 210). Thus, overall, the "generation at risk" idea applies as much to children being raised in marriages/families in which there is high conflict and low satisfaction experienced by the parents as it applies to children raised in single-parent households or by one or more stepparents.

Similar to Emery's (1999) claim, noted earlier, Amato (2000) reached the following conclusion in an overall summary article of work on children of divorce:

> *In conclusion, I return to the contentious debate over divorce that has continued throughout the 1990s. On one side are those who see divorce as an important contributor to many social problems. On the other side are those who see divorce as largely a benign force that provides adults with a second [or greater!] chance for happiness and rescues children from dysfunctional and aversive home environments. Based on the accumulated research of the 1990s—and of earlier decades—it is reasonable to conclude that both of these views represent one-sided accentuations of reality. The increase in marital instability has not brought society to the brink of chaos, but neither has it led to a golden age of freedom and self-actualization. Divorce benefits some individuals, leads others to experience temporary decrements in well-being that improve over time, and forces others on a downward cycle from which they might never fully recover. Continuing research on the contingencies that determine whether divorce has positive, neutral, or negative long-term consequences for adults and children is a high priority. (p. 1282)*

THE ROLE OF STARTER MARRIAGES IN THIS DIALOGUE

In the context of this ongoing dialogue about the effects of divorce on the children and the family, the concept of "starter marriage" (SM) is gaining some attention. Journalist Pamela Paul's book *The Starter Marriage and The Future of Matrimony* (2002) describes SMs as those involving no more than 5 years of marriage and no children, with the participants usually in their 20s or early 30s. Paul based her analysis on approximately 60 interviews with people experiencing SMs. In our marrying world, of course, almost all SM spouses expect to remarry, and most believe that they gained some perspective from these quick-and-out marriages. During their youth, many of these individuals experienced divorce in their families of origin, or their view of marriage was affected by divorce, affairs, and the like in families with whom they had close contact as they grew up.

Paul (2002) concluded that SMs are especially common among members of Generation X, who were born between 1965 and 1978 and who will thus be in their 30s in the early 21st century. She also believes that SMs may become similarly common among "Echo Boomers," born between 1979 and 1994. Paul believes Gen X people may be vulnerable to such marriages in part because they are very romantic: They believe in love at first sight, and SMs are built on too little experience with and information about one's partner, especially in terms of the partner's relationship tendencies. Paul suggested that Gen Xers yearn for a return to the "Leave it to Beaver" period, including "traditional parental responsibility" and even "traditional homemaking," more than Baby Boomers. She notes that Gen Xers use words like *family, stability, security,* and *lifelong love* in reference to what marriage means to them.

Paul (2002) argued there has been a politicization of marriage. Covenant marriage legislation, which makes divorce more difficult to obtain, are illustrative. She wrote the "marriage police" are omnipresent. In 2000, a marriage movement meeting attended by policy analysts, lawyers, clergy, judges, and other professionals was conducted with the goal of resanctifying marriage and discouraging divorce. A goal of this movement is to find 2 million married couples to serve as mentors for young couples. Paul implied logic similar to that of Constance Ahrons (1994) that there is an unfortunate labeling of divorce with terms such as *failed marriage* and *broken home*. She concluded that pro-marriage forces want people to get married but do not articulate very good "whys" and want people to stay married without much careful scrutiny of the "hows." She argued that the rationale of the pro-marriage movement is simplistic, biased, and nonempathic toward people divorcing; the movement does not adequately recognize the pain and distress (including as experienced in the bedroom, the most intimate area of interaction) those divorcing couples are experiencing. Thus, politics has become inextricably hooked into 21st-century marriage and divorce issues.

As Paul (2002) noted, there is room for much pessimism about divorce as a continuing issue in U.S. society. She quoted leading sociological divorce scholar Larry Bumpass: "The duration of [the divorce] trend suggests that the roots of current patterns of marital instability are deep, and not just a response to recent changes in other domains such as fertility, sex-role attitudes, female employment, or divorce laws" (Paul, 2002, pp. 175–176).

Paul's (2002) analysis feeds into the present book in her suggestion that many of the people in SMs have seen divorce "up close and personally" in their lives. Nonetheless, they are idealistic about the likelihood that their marriage will survive. That idealism frequently turns sour in the context of busy dual-career lives, which involve many early stressors, shattered dreams, and such logic as "getting out while you're still young" or "cutting your losses." Overall, Paul's SM story provides a further backdrop for understanding the development of young people's feelings regarding closeness and marriage.

DIVERSE SCHOLARLY VOICES

As is obvious from the preceding commentary, there is a cacophony of voices in the scholarly literature on the effects of divorce on children. In this chapter we have presented a quite selective sampling of these voices. We have discussed some major differences in the findings and conclusions advanced by these scholars. This state of affairs likely will persist as more scholars address this complex topic.

Just as is true in the narratives to follow, there is no absolutely well-established, consensually agreed-on position regarding the effects of divorce on children. Consistent with Emery's (1999) and Amato and Booth's (1997) conclusions, "it depends" resonates with the data as well as the reports presented in the chapters that follow. Amato and Booth's final conclusions about the research efforts needed to identify different magnitudes and types of divorce effects for adults and children are well taken. They believed that such work would occupy researchers for the first decade of the 20th century, and we believe that this work will take even longer to complete—if it ever is. One of the reasons that we believe that this work will take so long is that the effects of divorce are clearly contextualized, and it will take years to map out how individuals are affected by this wide range of contextual variables (e.g., sex of child, extent of involvement of the parents, visitation arrangements, socioeconomic status, and changes following divorce). For most of the children of divorce sampled in this literature, the matter of their parents' divorce is a changing target of perceived impact, interest, and angst over time. For some, it fades and may be perceived as ancient history. For others, it seems to live on for years and years. For still others, there are many in-between points in the memorial chain. What we greatly need is work on the models of marriage and family that young and middle-aged people regularly invoke and presumably use in their own close relationships. That need is implied in the narratives presented in this book.

RISK AND RESILIENCE

This book fits into the vast arena of work on risk and resilience among the young. There is an extensive literature on the topic of risk among the young people in families in which divorce occurs. As the foregoing literature suggests, there is a mix of opinion regarding how well children (younger and older) do in the context of diverse divorce circumstances. A general literature (e.g., Egeland, Carlson, & Stroufe, 1993; Luthar, 1991) has emerged suggesting that various types of interventions, such as counseling, early in the divorce process helps young people deal with the vagaries of their parents' divorce over an extended period. The work in general shows much hope for parents, educators, and counselors interested in enhancing young persons' resilience. As the respondents in this book suggest, children often have many positive assets that can be marshaled by caring adults to help them navigate even daunting divorce situations.

This hopeful tone of work on risk and resilience among the young is reinforced by a prominent movement in the behavioral sciences aimed at emphasizing positive outcomes (e.g., the positive psychology approach; Snyder & Lopez, 2002). We trust that this book will be seen as adding to that emphasis. Our work highlights the value of storytelling and giving voice to young people about the pain of divorce and to their special odysseys of adaptation to these divorce-related losses in their families.

WHY THE "LOSS AND GROWTH" THEME?

Related to the preceding discussion, this book speaks to the national debate about divorce and children of divorce in particular. The subtitle of *Stories of Loss and Growth* represents the overarching theme of the collection of stories. Many hearts are broken in divorce—hence the "loss." We should fear most the breaking of children's hearts. Nonetheless, with divorce a fact of life that likely will not just fade away, it is somewhat reassuring to hear the messages of these young people who ever so strongly show the other side of the coin: the growth. They represent individuals who recognize that there are no simple answers to the dilemmas of closeness, young adults who are ready to work with what they have and try to make the most of life given the cards they were dealt.

This book challenges the contention that most children of divorce will be irretrievably hurt by their parents' divorce. It will bring to bear a mixture of young people's voices, showing the great variety of reactions to parental divorce. It also will show the strength and resilience many of these young people have learned by having to pull themselves through the pain and confusion surrounding divorce in their families. It will show how hope and willingness to try to have stronger families themselves represent abiding themes in this sample of young persons.

> *There was a time when I thought I loved my first wife more than life itself. But now I hate her guts. I do. How do you explain that? What happened to that love?... I wish someone could tell me.*
> *(Carver, p. 133)*

2

THEORETICAL PERSPECTIVE AND METHODS

$\mathbf{A}$s we explicate in this chapter, the themes listed in Table 2.1 were developed in this project on the basis of evaluation of hundreds of student commentaries about their parents' divorces. The method used to gather the accounts reflecting these themes is discussed later in this chapter.

Beginning with chapter 3, this book revolves around college students' narrative accounts of their divorce-related experiences. In this chapter we provide a brief overview of the theoretical ap-

TABLE 2.1
Major Themes From Students' Narratives

- Pain and sadness (chap. 3)
- Hope (chap. 4)
- Becoming fatherless because of divorce (chap. 5)
- Family chaos and resilience (chap. 6)

proach that guided our decision to present these narrative accounts; describe the methods used to gather, analyze, and report the students' narrative accounts; and share some caveats regarding drawing inferences from these accounts.

AN ACCOUNT-MAKING THEORETICAL PERSPECTIVE

Behind the logic of this book is what John Harvey and his colleagues have referred to as an *account-making perspective* (e.g., Harvey, Weber, & Orbuch, 1990; Orbuch, 1997). To understand what we mean by an *account-making perspective* it is first important to realize that we are all storytellers; that is our bedrock capacity as human beings (Coles, 1989). As Bochner, Ellis, and Tillmann-Healy (1997) noted, people rely on stories to make sense out of their ongoing lived experience. Furthermore, stories both reflect the "objective" realities of what we experience and shape our interpretations of our experiences. Thus, stories both represent and shape experience (Bochner et al., 1997).

We all have in our memories a multitude of stories. As people share their stories with others, they name and shape the meanings of their unique life experience. They also pass on their heritage of stories to their confidants. When confidants or listeners become new tellers, they too reshape the original stories, incorporating their own particular issues and matters of moment. Thus, any given story is never retold in exactly the same way.

Particularly important to people's coping with life's stresses are narratives of loss and sharing parts of those narratives with close, caring others. A valuable tradition of scholarship exists in the area of people's storytelling about relationship loss (e.g., Ellis, 1995; Orbuch, 1997; Weiss, 1975). However, to our knowledge, this tradition has not been extended in the scholarly literature to narratives of children of divorce.

Harvey et al. (1990) defined *account-making* as "*the act of explaining, describing, and emotionally reacting to the major events in our lives in story-like form*" (p. 4). We suggest that this account-making often begins in our private reflections and then is communicated in the form of an account to other people in whom we confide. When a major loss occurs, confiding our feelings to close others becomes in time an essential act of coping and adaptation. As is often true, both persons in a confiding situation may be telling stories of loss and comforting one another. It is the reciprocal communicative act that makes this experience a powerfully social event and, as noted earlier, this act has implications for both the listener and the teller. As we suggest in this book, meaning- and account-making and confiding about our grief to close others are among our most significant tools for confronting, understanding, and addressing our losses. In essence, that is what the young people are doing in providing their stories in this book. Furthermore, and to our good fortune, not only do the students have the potential to benefit from telling their divorce-related stories, but also we, as part of the scholarly community, have the opportunity to learn from their experiences as reflected in their narrative accounts.

As we discuss further later, it is important to realize that the students' stories do not reflect external reality in an absolute sense; in contrast, stories are influenced by the individuals' values, attitudes, perspectives, and preferences. Where do these values, attitudes, and so forth, come from? Bochner et al. (1997) distinguished between *canonical* and *personal* stories. Canonical narratives reflect the socially acceptable story in a particular culture, such as that married people should live happily ever after. Personal stories, by contrast, are those that individuals choose to construct and share with others. Bochner et al. suggested that personal stories are often created in such a way that they work to counteract the constraints of canonical conventions. As Bochner et al. stated, "Many personal narratives attempt to authorize and/or legitimate marginalized, exceptional or particular experiences. These narratives function as oppositional stories that seek to reform or transform canonical ones" (p. 315). In this book, we report students' personal narratives, but we recognize that these stories are written in response to students' perceptions of canonical wisdom. Thus, in their stories, students often responded to their interpretation of social convention, such as what they had heard from guest speakers in class; popular literature, such as Wallerstein and Blakeslee's (2003) recent book; their image of how nuclear families are supposed to function; or their view of how a "good" divorce plays itself out. Thus, when reading the students' stories, we ask readers to keep in mind that they are seeing personal narratives that are influenced by cultural scripts regarding family-related phenomena, such as relationships, relationship loss, family interactions, and divorce.

YOUNG PERSONS' VOICES:
HOW WERE THEIR STORIES GATHERED AND ANALYZED?

The stories, or excerpts from stories, presented in the following chapters were chosen from more than 900 narratives presented in John Harvey's classes in the middle to late 1990s until 2002. How were the stories generated? Undergraduate students (mean age = 21, with a small percentage of nontraditional students in each class) in two of John Harvey's courses—"Close Relationships" and "Loss and Trauma"—at the University of Iowa (both upper division classes), students who indicated that their parents had divorced were asked to write as much as they wanted to regarding the pros and cons of the divorce for all parties concerned. They were encouraged to tell how the divorce affected them and their siblings and to give specific details. These writing exercises occurred partially in the 75-min class, but students also were allowed to complete the narrative at their own pace outside of class. This narrative work occurred after discussion in the class of the "children of divorce" literature (a topic that was covered to some extent in each course), approximately 1 month into each term.

To make sense of the large number of narratives, Harvey worked with four graduate students to identify categories of narratives over the more than 5 years when these student narratives were collected. They identified four categories of narratives, which were approximately equal in prominence: a) those that emphasized negative themes (presented in chap. 3, on despair), b) those that emphasized positive themes (presented in chap. 4, on hope), c) those that emphasized "missing a parent" (presented in chap. 5, on a lack of father involvement), and d) those that emphasized family dysfunction and adaptation (presented in chap. 6, on family chaos and resilience).

As will be obvious to readers who closely examine the narratives in chapters 3 through 6, there was overlap among the categories, reflecting the complex nature of the experience; few of the students' experiences could be classified as purely positive or negative in nature. We recognize this overlap and believe that it is unavoidable given the vastness and vagaries of the divorce experience in these students' lives. It will be clear to readers that these classifications sometimes are not even close to precise. As a reviewer of this work rightly noted, "any classification of such material may oversimplify the nuances, subtleties, complexities, and contradictions of individual reactions to parental divorce." For this reason, we present the vast majority of narratives in their complete form, as a means of attempting to reflect these nuances, subtleties, and complexities in the students' experiences.

Harvey and the graduate students identified sets of the most representative 10–20 stories per category and then ordered them in terms of purity/potency of theme. The best exemplars of these themes were chosen for further discussion among the coders, with the ones chosen for presentation here rated as the most informative. Disagreements among raters were discussed until agreement was reached. The stories considered to best exemplify each category are presented in the relevant chapter.

We should emphasize that the narratives were collected under the agreement that they might be a part of this presentation. All names and other clearly identifying information have been changed to protect the identities of the individuals. Furthermore, these narratives were collected as an ancillary, optional task in university-approved research in Harvey's classes.

As much as possible, the stories are presented in raw form, even with grammatical imperfections. Students were not graded for literacy; they often were writing quickly to present as much information as they could in the context of many other demands on their time; many of these narratives contain numerous instances of ungrammatical sentences and misspelled words. As will be seen, however, some narratives were extraordinarily well written and obviously required much time in reflection and composition. To enhance the authenticity of presentation, we believe that it is essential to show the narratives in their basic form of exposition. Only in a few cases where sentences were so ungrammatical that meaning was jeopardized was minimal editing done. Some stories are fairly long and intact; others are short and abbreviated. We strongly believe that reporting the narratives in their original, unaltered form best captures the nuanced and sometimes subtle meaning of these students' experiences.

CAVEATS ON DRAWING INFERENCES
FROM THE NARRATIVE ACCOUNTS

It is important that we provide readers with some caveats regarding drawing inferences from the students' narrative accounts of their divorce-related experiences. By way of context, we note, as we did in chapter 1, that we agree with Emery's (1999) conclusions that divorce is stressful for children, that divorce increases children's risk of having adjustment problems, that most children are resilient in coping with divorce, that divorce involves considerable pain and leads to unpleasant memories, and that the nature of postdivorce family interactions plays an important role in determining how effectively children cope with divorce.

Our concordance with Emery's (1999) conclusions leads to several caveats regarding the drawing of inferences from the students' accounts. First, by its very nature, divorce is a process inextricably intertwined with the experience of loss. Thus, it is not surprising that a major, if not *the* major, theme from the remaining part of the book is one of pain, grief, and sadness. Even when "positive" aspects of the divorce experience are described in the narratives, these aspects are often reported in the context of unpleasant or unhappy experiences. However, our understanding of the literature suggests that reports of unpleasant memories and pain do not necessarily indicate that the individual has experienced significant adjustment problems. Rather, given the resilience noted by Emery (1999), we would expect that most of the students who have reported on painful divorce-related experiences are relatively well adjusted.

Second, even though we have argued that individuals' narrative accounts are embedded with meaning and significance, we also caution readers that the stories are reflective of only one person's perspective at a particular time. Other family members may have very different memories and views of the divorce perspective. Thus, readers should not conclude that the students' recollections are necessarily accurate in the sense of being veridical with "objective" reality. Thus, the stories should be read with the goal of acquiring a sense of the students' unique phenomenological experience rather than to determine which events actually occurred.

Third, the students are reporting on their parents' divorces when they are in their early 20s. Will they have the same perceptions and entertain the same opinions 10, 20, and 30 years into the future regarding these divorces? We do not know, but we suspect that they will not. Perceptions of the divorce process very likely will change over time, partly because new experiences will lead individuals to rethink and reconstruct some of their memories and opinions related to the divorce. However, how much change there will be, and in what directions, is difficult to discern. No solid evidence on this matter exists to our knowledge. Nevertheless, we argue that the students' stories are still instructive for those of us trying to understand divorce, because they represent their thinking at the time and because the meanings that they attach to their divorce-related experiences at such an influential time have important effects (on themselves and on others) throughout their lifetimes.

Fourth, the young people whose stories are presented in this book may not represent all young people everywhere who cope with their parents' divorces. These people, in the main, came from White, middle-class families. We do not know if the reports of people from other ethnic and socioeconomic backgrounds would reflect the same themes and conclusions. There is a desperate need for more information on how divorce is experienced by and affects individuals from other ethnic and minority groups. In addition, these respondents also were studying divorce as part of their undergraduate work in Harvey's "Close Relationships" and "Loss and Trauma" courses at the University of Iowa. This experience alone makes them different from other young people who have experienced their parents' divorce and, consequently, they then might form different positions on the merits of the divorce. In addition, although Mark Fine has not elicited detailed narratives from his students in his "Process of Divorce" class at the University of Missouri, some of the stories he has heard from students in their written work and from class discussions are interspersed throughout the book. These students, too, may not be representative of the population of all individuals who have experienced parental divorce.

An important caveat is that the request for students to provide their stories may have led to perceptions (and, eventually, stories) that otherwise are not a part of their ongoing experience of their parents' divorces. In particular, respondents in the later years of this project had probably heard about Wallerstein, Lewis, and Blakeslee's (2000b) argument that, for many children of divorce, it would be better if parents stayed in marriages that may have been unhappy but that did not involve high levels of conflict. This argument formed one important foil against which many respondents reacted.

Another backdrop for comments in the narratives were discussions in classes by panels of students who were reporting on their experiences with divorce in their own families. These students represented a continuum of types of divorces, from horrible to quite civil and resolved. They also showed differences in how well they had adapted to the divorces. Their lively stories often brought out reactions by students writing their narratives.

A final caveat is that, without exposure to the findings and theories from the dissolution literature, students very likely would not have advanced points in their stories that were explicitly linked to research and theory. Furthermore, other children of divorce who have not been exposed to this literature may present different descriptions of and attributions about the dynamics of divorce in their families.

Even with these major caveats to consider, we believe that the stories presented in this book provide a useful perspective about young people's experiences of their parents' divorces. To our knowledge, no available work in the literature contains this many stories from children of divorce. Even though the themes reported are likely to be fairly universal, the many nuances shown are likely to be only suggestive of the vastness of experience that may be found among the millions of young people whose parents have divorced.

OUR HOPE

We hope that the special emphasis on the personal voices of the children of divorce will make these narratives useful to scholars, practitioners, students, and parents. We hope that this method of stressing the raw input of respondents will make the experiences more vivid and realistic—if sometimes visceral and unpleasant at the same time—to readers. In the end, we hope that this type of approach will enhance both understanding of and compassion for children of divorce and for the parents who diligently try to make their children's welfare the highest priority in their postdivorce lives.

CHAPTER

3

VOICES OF DESPAIR

For me divorce means more than a legal dissolution. It means heartache, change, negative thoughts and feelings.

—From a young man's report in this chapter

Unlike the more hopeful messages portrayed in the next chapter, the presentations in this chapter reveal different patterns of turmoil, lost courses in life, and general despair. Although there are mixtures of gain and hope in the remarks contained herein, this chapter is dedicated to stories that emphasize these unpleasant qualities. The despair, feelings of confusion, and anger registered by the commentators in this chapter rival the types of loss perceived by people in Wallerstein et al.'s (2000b) book. Many respondents also note the behavioral patterns of chaos and craziness that flow in their lives, in part because of their parents' decision to divorce. These stories also relate closely to those in chapter 5 on becoming "fatherless," as many of these students strongly feel the absence of a parent in their lives.

The central themes of this chapter are presented in Table 3.1. As shown in the table, these themes were mostly bleak and ranged from reports of experiencing raw pain to changes in beliefs and perspective regarding relationships (e.g., becoming cynical about romantic relationships, a shattering of beliefs in the perfect family).

The first story, by a 20-year-old female, addresses the raw emotion of shock and disillusionment associated with her parents' divorce.

SHOCK AND DISILLUSIONMENT

When I was growing up, or at least where I was growing up, divorce was still taboo. "Normal" kids had two parents who lived in the same house. My parents were married for 15 years, 8 of which were happy, claims my mom. The details of their marriage were never made apparent to my brother and I, we just knew that they were happy. Now that I am 20 and my parents have been divorced for almost 8 years, I am a little more enlightened.

My mom got pregnant and married shortly after, when she was 19 and my father was 20. My parents had known each other for 2 months before the pregnancy, and 6 months before the marriage. It was the true definition of a shotgun wedding. However, growing up, I knew none of this and never would have guessed any of it. My parents were the happiest couple I knew. I never imagined that they were forced into their marriage.

When my parents got divorced, I went into shock. Divorce affects every child differently. My brother, for instance, became very distant and cold to-

TABLE 3.1
Major Themes of Despair From Students' Narratives

- Shock and disillusionment
- End of the "perfect family"
- Financial and visitation difficulties
- Children feeling stuck in the middle between sometimes-angry parents or ex-spouses
- Deep sadness about the ripping away of the family fabric
- Becoming cynical about relationships in general and their own close relationships
- Experience of raw pain by children of divorced parents

ward my mother. He chose not to express any emotion. He removed himself from the situation. I, on the other hand, became very sad. I didn't understand, because as I said, their marriage was perfect. I withdrew from my friends, I couldn't sleep, and I cried all of the time.

I think that one thing you learn by being a child of divorce is that relationships are work. I asked my parents time and time again, "Can't you just try harder?" I finally understood that they had tried extremely hard for the last 5 years of their relationship. There comes a point though, when it's too much work and not enough love. That is not a relationship worth validating.

I find that children of divorce almost inevitably relate their parents' divorce to their own romantic relationships, and possibly other relationships. For instance, when my parents got divorced, I swore that if I had children, I would never get divorced. This may be an extremely naive way of thinking considering the divorce rates in our country, however, maybe not. One way of looking at this view is that, I am going to be extremely careful in all of my romantic relationships. If I am dating someone, they have to possess qualities that I will be able to live with, and that I will be able to depend on. I know that I will not say "I do" if I am not one-hundred percent sure that this is the person I want, and can spend the rest of my life with. My marriage will not be for convenience or spontaneous; it will be well thought out. I may still get divorced, but at least I can say that I tried my hardest to make it work.

On the other hand, my brother now has both a fear of being alone, and a fear of commitment. He ends relationships by starting a new one with someone else. I think this has a lot to do with my parents' divorce. My roommate, whose mom has been divorced three times, has been with the same guy for 4 years and will marry him some day. How we children of divorce approach our relationships is due largely to our parents' relationships and how we handled their divorce. I think that children of divorce experience a shock of reality and disillusionment that they can not prepare for. This one event will continue to influence their lives on many levels. I know it has for me.

Comment

This disillusionment has also been shown in indirect ways by Mark Fine's students in their discussions of the effects of divorce. In the beginning of Fine's "Process of Divorce" class, students are asked to write a position paper on the topic of whether divorce should be made easier or more difficult to obtain. At this early stage of the course, most students, even those whose parents are still married, argue that divorce should be made more difficult to obtain. To justify their position, students whose parents had divorced cited several consequences of their parents' divorce that they considered to be "long-term," such as having to grow up too quickly, becoming angry with or distant from one or both parents, suffering financial losses, and having a cynical view of the prospects for romantic relationships working out well. By the end of the course many of these students had changed their position on this topic, arguing that divorce should either be made easier to obtain or that it, at least, should not be made more difficult to obtain.

END OF "THE PERFECT FAMILY"

As will be seen in these narratives, for some students the divorce occurred at a somewhat distant point in their relatively short lives. For others, however, it was quite recent. The pain in the latter stories is palpable. In this first report, a 20-year-old man describes some of the hurt and feelings of loss that he has felt since the decision of his parents to divorce in the last 3 years.

My parents had been separated for about 6 months, so the announcement of their divorce did not really surprise me. What hit me hard, though, was the finality of the decision. All hope of Mom and Dad getting back together was taken away in the span of a few minutes during our "family meeting."

I was always a quiet child. I was the kind of kid that friends' parents liked because I was polite and conscientious. I followed the rules, was never late coming home, and homework always came before baseball practice. So, without trying to sound conceited, I was a pretty good kid....

My best friend once told me that he thought I had the perfect family. When my parents were together, it seemed that way. We had a nice house, went on vacations, and did normal things. The details of why my parents got divorced are not important to me. In fact, I still do not know all the reasons. What I do know is that their divorce sparked this anger inside me that I could not control. I was not so angry at my parents because I saw the pain they were in. I had built up rage inside me, such that I did not know what to do. My grades went to hell. I started to cause trouble, which was probably a cry for attention. I got in trouble with the police several times. I had major temper tantrums.

I look back now a couple of years later and am embarrassed by my actions. My family thought I was crazy. Whenever my Mom left the house, I would look out the window, sometimes for hours, waiting for her to come home. I guess I thought that she wasn't coming home.

During this period, I'd be lucky if I slept 4 hours a night. Late one night, I overheard my mom talking to my older brother about me. She knew I was miserable. My mom and dad sat me down and told me that they wanted me to see a psychologist. That just made me angry. They dropped the idea, but I could see I was hurting them. Looking back, I may have wanted to hurt them—they were the ones getting divorced.

As more time passed, I began to calm down a lot. I started to feel better about things. My life started to come back together. That is, it seemed to be until my mom had her first date, but that's another story. I'm glad I wrote this. It was the first time I have expressed these feelings all together. I had managed to keep them inside, and it hurt.

Comment

The foregoing report resonates with accounts from many of the respondents who provided stories for this project. These stories speak to the feelings of pain and loss at the fracturing of a family that seemed "normal" and intact, but all of a sudden, the family was no longer of whole cloth. Rather, the individual has a new set of realities to negotiate, one that does not seem "normal," much less perfect, anymore. It is a world filled with new contingencies in traveling to visit a noncustodial parent, in encountering new economic difficulties, and in experiencing embarrassment in interacting with friends or with others whom they believe will view them negatively because of the divorce in their family. Then, this new world also may involve having to soon deal with a parent's dating behavior and even the possibility of having to begin to understand what it is like to be in a blended family.

In the following account, a 22-year-old man describes the loss of his family as the loss of illusions about the perfect family and how his family would remain together throughout his life. His story is similar to the stories of many people who stressed the importance, or even sacredness, of family to them—especially after witnessing a life of "hell" in their divorcing families. These young people often advanced the idea that because they had seen so much ugliness in the divorcing situations in their families, they felt not only insecure in their own close relationships but also more dedicated to making their relationships work.

Family is very important to me and always has been. From the time I was a young boy, I've always enjoyed the warm embrace of a loved one. Throughout history in many cultures family has been looked upon as the center of our lives, and represents our well-being. During the early and mid 1900s marriage was looked upon as, "till death [do] us part." Getting a divorce was seen as a sign of weakness and considered taboo in American culture. Many people saw marriage as part of the American dream, which included two kids a car and a house. I had always felt that I was living in that dream, "the perfect life" until one day I heard the words that so many kids fear.

My parents symbolize to me what the American dream was believed to be in the early 1960s. My parents were high school sweethearts that met through mutual friends. They started dating when my father was a junior in high school and my mother was a freshman. My mom describes my dad at the time as the most generous, well-mannered person she had ever met. It was interesting when they started dating because my mother came from a blue-collar family and my dad's parents were very well off, but the interesting part is that my dad's dad was my mom's dad's boss at work. They had worked together since my parents were very young children. My parents dated until my mom graduated high school and then they decided to get married. After getting married they decided to move from their parents' houses in southern Illinois to the Chicago area to go to school and find jobs. Soon after moving to the Chicago area they had received their first bad news that my dad had been drafted to the Vietnam war. They moved back to southern Illinois, said their goodbyes and didn't know if they'd ever see each other again. They say it was one of the hardest things they'd ever have to go through, as much as it brought them apart they say they had never felt closer. Thank God for me he survived his tour and when he returned they moved back to Chicago, started going to school, and my dad got a good job at major television station as a cameraman. Then they decided it was time to start our family, soon after my brother was born in the early 70s.

All my life I had grown up to believe that family and friends were all you needed in life to feel happy. I grew up the youngest of three children in middle to upper class suburb of Chicago. I have a brother who is quite a bit older and a sister who's 5 years older than me. We grew up in a neighborhood surrounded with friends. I remember my parents throwing parties with friends and family and all the good times we'd have together. We had a very close relationship with our neighbors, we would all go on vacations together or spend the weekends at somebody's lake house. My parents always stressed how important it was to be around the people you love.

My mom is a very friendly lady who has worked as a nurse since I was a young boy. She has always had a very nurturing personality and a sort of calming effect on people's emotions. I believe nursing was her calling to life. When I was young, I would wrap myself in her robe while she was away at work because I'd miss her so much. My dad had started his own business when we were all young and it continued to prosper up until he sold it when I was in junior high. I've always been proud to say he's my father; he is very good to all of us and enjoyed bringing us to the pool and just being with us whenever he wasn't working. He even employed all my brother's and sister's friends to work for him; I would help out by bringing out the trash or just wasting time around his office. We all looked up to him and felt that he was a great father. People always had the utmost respect for him because of how he always made it to church on Sundays and treated everyone with respect. He was very friendly to all of our friends and so corny in a way that he would make you laugh.

When I was growing up it seemed like almost everyone's parents had been divorced or were on their second marriages. It made me proud to say that my parents had been married for 28 years. I always felt like I kind of had an edge because I had the support of two loving parents that had been married for as long as they had been. They had been together for so long that it never seemed like they could break up, they were too old. One day during the summer before my junior year of high school my dad woke me up and said that we needed to talk. What I heard next are words that I feel still affect me to this day. He told me that things hadn't been working out between him and my mom for awhile and they were going to get "a divorce." When I first heard it I think I was in shock and didn't completely understand the consequences.

My first thought was really kind of a numb feeling. I obviously wasn't happy, but on the other hand I don't remember being sad. I don't know if I was being selfish at the time or if it just really didn't bother me on the outside because the first thing I could think of is if it's only my mom living at home it will be so much easier on me. My dad was always the one that was hard on us about grades and curfew, and my mom was the more easygoing type. Then I went through a period were I was mad at my dad; I blamed him for the divorce because it was his idea. I felt like I didn't have to listen to him and anything he said didn't really mean as much to me. I thought he had lied to our whole family and kind of disgraced us. My brother and sister were both living away from home so I really couldn't talk to them about it, but even though they were older we still talk about it today how it made us angry, as though we'd been let down. I felt almost embarrassed to tell my friends because like I said before I had always felt that a solid family life represented to them who or what I was about. It made me feel strong and good about myself, and now this web of family support that I had once had was torn apart and my once perfect world was no longer.

I played it off to my parents and everyone else that it really didn't affect me that much. I held a lot of the feeling inside, and didn't want to really let anyone in on how I truly felt because I thought it made me look bad. Although many people experience divorce I felt my experience was disenfranchised grief [grief that is not well recognized or supported in society], because I couldn't open up to anyone because of the way it made me feel about myself and my family. I believe I was to caught up on how it looked to other people, because my parents had always talked about other families who were getting divorced. When I say families I feel that way because a divorce doesn't only affect the people involved in the marriage it affects those who surround the family as well.

It wasn't until football started that I started to feel the pressures of the divorce. I was a returning starter on varsity and still I began to lose focus and not care as much about playing football anymore. Sports were one of the things that my dad and I had in common, and he was one of my driving forces for doing well. He would always practice with me and tell me I did a good job regardless of how I felt I did. At this point a couple of weeks after telling me they were getting a divorce I had lost focus and wanted to do other things that didn't cause me stress. At one point I couldn't take the pressure of practice and playing along with school, so I had hoped that I would get hurt, so I could do what I wanted. Well 2 weeks into the season the stress had taken its toll on my back and I couldn't play because I had two pinched nerves in my lower back. I didn't have to worry about playing for the next 3 weeks, but now I had a back problem. It began what I consider a pileup of losses. First the divorce, which caused me stress so I didn't feel I could focus on anything, then I hurt my back, which caused me even more stress because it hurt to walk, and finally after all this I felt as though I had let myself down. I couldn't deal with all that was going on in my life at such a critical age of 16. In 2 months I had gone from the best time of my life to losing all the support I had once felt.

The breakup gave me a sense of distrust toward my father because of all the things he had taught us growing up. I would ask myself how a person who goes to church every Sunday, has three children, and a wife who has lived nearly her whole life with him could do this. I believe my father was ashamed of what he did and couldn't tell his own parents, my only living grandparents, because of his beliefs. I don't think he wanted to let them know he failed or let them down because they're very old fashioned. My father was raised very Catholic and shortly after this had happened he stopped going to the Catholic Church because I feel he thought it is wrong to get divorced. He's seeing another lady now and has begun going to another non-denominational church because I think he is trying to justify his actions that they're not wrong. I think his new church is more accepting of how he lives his life.

I believe this experience has affected me in many ways. For example, I know that over the past couple of relationships I have felt less secure, which I believe has led me to act out in more jealous and less trusting ways. This type of behavior can turn a good relationship bad for no apparent reason. I tend to hold back on letting someone know how I feel about them because I'm more fearful of being hurt. I sometimes jump to conclusions or try to read the other person's mind to interpret how they're feeling, sometimes coming up with a negative response. I sometimes feel that I could have done so much more with athletics and school had I not lost that confidence and desire to succeed that I had once felt. When I was first deciding were I would go away to college I had always wanted to go to one of the coasts. I wanted to see what's outside of the Midwest, but since my mom is still single I've kind of always felt that she needed us around her, so I've put my plans on hold. In a sense the breakup has put a more needy strain on our relationship. I worry about her well-being and health and don't want to see her lonely. She's a very strong woman, but she grew up in a large family and has always needed that support around her. I grew up with this feeling of invincibility that has since been somewhat suppressed; I think the whole event of loss makes you realize your human and bad things do happen to good people.

Finally, I want you to realize that many bad things do come out of loss, but there are many things that can make you stronger from it as well. From the experience I have learned that the human spirit may bend, but it will never break and as hard as things may be they can help make you a stronger person. I've learned a lot about myself, that many of the ways I used to think and feel were just the way a young adult looks at life. I've matured in so many ways that I look back at the things I used to do or say and thank God things didn't get worse. Through all the hard times I always kept a level head and that gives me confidence for the future. At times it may seem that I'm being irrational in my thinking, but like you said everyone deals with loss differently. Through time, now more than ever I'm thankful that

I have two loving parents, and although I'd love to see them together, I can accept that we're all together apart. Like so many other people today I've seen the end of that dream, "the perfect life" and awakened to the reality that life goes on, and sometimes what seems to hurt the most only makes you stronger.

Comment

This case nicely illustrates the interweaving of both the best and the worst of divorce- related consequences. On the one hand, this young man vividly describes how painful and devastating it was to have his parents divorce after so many years of marriage. His pain and distress were so acute that he lost "focus" and the ability to concentrate on previously familiar activities, such as football. Even now, after the acute distress has apparently abated, the divorce still has undesirable consequences, such as influencing his level of trust in his own romantic relationships and restricting his autonomy to relocate to another part of the country (i.e., to support his mother). On the other hand, he very clearly states that he believes that the divorce made him stronger and perhaps more mature. We placed this narrative in the Despair chapter because of the raw pain this young man experienced, but his story also nicely illustrates the wide range of nuanced feelings and reactions that young people have as they negotiate their parents' divorce.

FINANCIAL AND VISITATION DIFFICULTIES

The newly divorced often suffer from money woes—how could it be otherwise when people carve up what they had and might not have had that much to begin with? Children of divorce quickly mention economic difficulties. They often experience difficulty in affording items that they previously could easily purchase. They often have trouble with school expenses or in owning or servicing an automobile. As is true in the following account, written by a 21-year-old woman, they also frequently mention the difficulties associated with visitation after divorce.

My parents separated when I was in my freshmen year of college. My mom was the one that told me the week before spring break that he was going to move out over spring break. Luckily, I had a road trip planned with my friends for the week so I wouldn't be there. It seems like that was one of the only reprieves from the loss of the divorce, because it was certainly painful to live in my house when my parents were together and after my parents separated I felt a different kind of hurt.

My parents didn't have a good relationship for a long time before the separation actually happened. My dad has a very bad temper and was physically and emotionally abusive mostly to my sisters and me, but sometimes he was definitely emotionally abusive to my mother. I didn't have a good relationship with my dad while I was growing up. Actually, there were times when I hated him, for what he did to me and what he did to my family. I wanted my mom to leave my dad for about 10 years before it actually took place. I was pretty vocal about it too. Every time my mom and I would go shopping together, we talked about my dad and I told her how I felt. In the beginning, she was really hopeful that he would change, but after awhile she acknowledged that she was not happy. She was scared, though, of being on her own as a single mom of three young girls. She said that she wanted to stay with him for us; even though I refuted that [that] was worse, she still thought that. Finally, as I said, when I was 18, my mom told my dad he needed to move out. She had fallen out of love years ago, but it took 10 years to prepare her emotionally and financially and to get up the courage to change the status quo.

My dad moved out of our house and into a house 20 minutes away. It took nearly a year to get the divorce finalized because my parents had to haggle over money and visitation. That year was tough, because it was kind of like my family was in limbo. Nothing was cut and dry and there was no closure. My dad kept trying to come back into my mom's life. He even used us kids to find out about what my mom was doing.

During this year, it was hard figure out how to act. For my dad, it was no longer appropriate for him to just walk into the house. He was never really good at knocking. He would always just walk right in and it made me feel like my privacy was violated. My mom had a hard time interacting with my dad because he was always trying to be affectionate with her, which made it awkward. When my dad came over to our house, the conversation was stressed and I really didn't know what to talk about that was neutral. I wasn't really ever confused because I never had a good relationship with my dad so it didn't feel like I was missing anything when he left, and the bond between my mom and I just grew stronger.

Two of the biggest conflicts in a divorce are visitation and finances, which was completely true in my family. Since I was 18, I was an adult and never mandated to spend time with my dad. My dad was supposed to have both of my sisters every other weekend and on Wednesdays for dinner. My middle sister, however, did not have a good relationship with my dad and never wanted to go. She was old enough that he couldn't really force her, because she would just hate him. She never went with him and so after a couple months, he gave up. He still sees my youngest sister usually when he is supposed to.

Probably the biggest battle my parents had and continue to fight about is money. Every 6 months since the divorce, my parents are back in court reassessing child support based on salary and bills. It is just a big hassle for both of them. My dad is never current on paying the bills either so my mom has to always bug him to pay her.

Divorce is one of the most painful losses I have experienced in my lifetime and I was fortunate to think it was the best thing that could happen. It would have been even more painful if I hadn't understood why they were separating.

Children of divorced parents often are exposed to intimate details of their parents' financial situations—much more than they would be privy to had their parents remained married, and probably more than is in their best interests to know. One student in Mark Fine's "Process of Divorce Class" wrote the following:

Before the divorce, we were fairly well off, living in a nice house and getting most of what we wanted. After the divorce, my mother, my sister, and I moved into a small 2-bedroom apartment that was not even close to as nice as our former house. My parents argued a lot about the financial aspects of the divorce settlement and many of these arguments were in front of me. As a result, I became more aware than I wanted to of how child support was determined in Missouri. After the settlement, both of my parents felt that they had been treated unfairly and both claimed to be "poor." All I cared about was that it seemed that there wasn't any money to buy things with and this was all that much harder to deal with because, before the divorce, I had gotten used to getting what I wanted. The biggest changes I noticed following divorce were in the kind of place we lived in and the lack of having enough money to go around.

On the other hand, the following story, by a man, age 22, suggests that money is not everything. He and his family remain relatively affluent. Still, in the long run, as told by this young man, happiness remains elusive for this family, which tries to be civil but reveals much dysfunction and sorrow.

My sophomore year in high school was a little rough. First thing was that I was going to a private school 45 minutes from my home, and it wasn't the school I wanted to be going to either. Also my family was finishing up our dream home that we had been building for a year. This house was over a million dollars, and as you will quickly see, all the money in the world can't buy happiness. This house would cause my parents to get a divorce. At this time my parents had been married for almost 19 years and had dated since their freshman year in high school. There was no way this could be happening to my parents. But the day of the closing, my father was late to the house to sign the papers. He had been out drinking with some buddies, and showed up over 3 hours late. This is where two different stories come into play. My father claims that he walked in and saw the builder sitting next to my mother drinking a beer with his hand on her leg. My mother said that whatever he saw was completely innocent and that she didn't even remember it happening. This caused a huge argument that for a month they didn't speak to each other. They finally decided to try and be civil, but this only lasted for about 2 weeks. From then on, they slept in different sides of the house and never spoke unless to argue. Never really tried to fix it or reconcile in therapy. One night in particular, my father was watching TV right outside of my bedroom while I was playing PlayStation. Suddenly, they got into [it] right there in the hallway; to this day I don't know if they knew I was in my room. Everything came out in that argument, and it was the most disgusting thing I have ever heard. Not only was this a divorce, but there was a lot of money on both sides, which made it even uglier. From the time that they got separated to when the divorce was finalized was about 3 years. They had both moved out, dad started dating again, over a hundred appearances in court, and one nationally televised Dateline edition was aired. That was a little tough. It was very hard to go to school and have people ask me questions about my parents' divorce, and I didn't even know that it had been shown or even existed. You could imagine my surprise. The funny thing is that I really don't know why my parents actually got divorced and I have never asked. From what I know, that misunderstanding was the cause. My parents never really fought, except for maybe one little argument a year, but I imag-

ine that is normal in a marriage. The other weird thing was that I never cried. I feel crying at one point would have been a natural reaction, but I never did. In fact, I never really got upset about it. I was never sat down by either one of my parents, and I never asked them anything about it. I looked at it as my parents' business, and the less I knew the better. The only time it bothered me was the very first Christmas Eve after they moved out. My mother has a very large family, and my dad was one of them. My father even looked at my mother's father as more of a dad than his own. My dad was a buddy with my mom's brothers and it was very weird not hearing my dad make smart-ass remarks with my uncles. I have even heard stories that my dad and my mom's brothers would go out drinking together on Saturday nights, they would all hit on other women together, and the wives knew about it and did nothing. In fact, all the families and kids would get together every Sunday and relax together, and nothing would ever be said about the night before. As you can see, no one in this story is as happy as they were before the story of divorce began, or even before the house was being built. So after all, money isn't everything, and sometimes simply talking can do wonders.

IN THE MIDDLE

Probably no issue is as imposing to children of divorce as is the one of feeling stuck in the middle between angry ex-spouses. In this account, a 22-year-old woman describes how difficult it is for her and her siblings to be in the middle of an ugly divorce, the effects of which continue 4 years after they began.

One week after my 16th birthday, over family supper, my parents told my brother, my sister and me that they were getting a divorce. This night would prove to have an amazing impact on the rest of my life.

The last 4 years of my life have been a confusing, painful, and intense experience. As the oldest, I continue to feel responsible for the events that unfold in my family. I still feel the need to protect my sister and brother from the extreme chaos and turbulence forced onto us.

The divorce was anything but civil. Soon my mom and dad refused to talk to each other, using us as the go-between. Besides constantly being in the middle of arguments and bickering, other problems appeared. My dad all of a sudden decided to become the involved father that I'd never had. A large part of the problem lied in the fact that my dad had no idea about parenting, my mother had been totally in charge of our day to day life. The discipline problems were the only aspect in which my father ever dealt. His strict, new rules and policies did not sit well with the 16-year-old daughter that he had never really taken the time to get to know.

While this was going on, my mother's self-esteem plummeted as she slipped into a deep depression. This was probably the most difficult part. For various reasons, all of her friends deserted her at once. This simply increased her feeling of loneliness and anger, and isolation. Because we were around, we bore most of my mom's frustrations. My mother would become angry and lash out at us. As the oldest child and the one with the shortest fuse, I caught the worst.

After our massive fights, I would be riddled with guilt. I knew that as soon as I left she would start in on my brother or sister. Oftentimes they would be angry with me for starting a conflict, but it is against my nature to let the stunts my mother pulled go unnoticed. She was going through a period of regression, acting like a teenager with her newfound freedom. I felt the need to let her know that her immature, reckless behavior was not acceptable with me.

These battles with my mother became normal. I dreaded going home, realizing that conflict with her was inevitable. This was incredibly stressful for me. When it came time for me to go away to college, I was ecstatic. I was embarking on a normal life, away from the dysfunction that was an everyday occurrence for me. But at the same time I was torn, scared at how much more our family life would deteriorate for my siblings once I was not there to police my mother.

Although college offered a certain amount of distance, the aftermath of the divorce still plagued me. I still had my father putting me in the middle, giving me a threatening message to pass along to my mother. In addition, the occasional screaming match with my mom still occurred; the only difference was that I was yelling at the telephone. Although the worst would have to be the times where my 14-year-old brother would call, crying about something that happened. Those incidents would tear me up inside; I felt incredibly helpless. I was not able to fix things, or even try as I usually did.

Incidents indirectly resulting from the divorce forced me to come home for winter break early last year. The family needed me; I was told that my brother and sister needed me to be the strong one. However, I was an emotional mess. Anxiety overwhelmed me, and I cried constantly. After a few weeks, I needed to distance myself. I returned to school but became very depressed. I learned how to set boundaries with my family and keep a healthy distance for my own health.

Other grievances I hold with the divorce are my reluctant involvement. My parents treated me like a third party in the divorce. They made me much more aware than a teenager should be about the dirty details of the divorce. I would have been much happier if they would have let me be a kid, oblivious of what happened. They forced me to grow up much too quickly, making me shoulder much of the burden.

Now that more time has passed, situations have improved. Everyone in my family is more comfortable with current circumstances. And although the memories and pain will fade, the experience will impact me for the rest of my life. Like the average child of divorce, I am pessimistic about marriage and do not want children of my own. But I appear to display more negative effects. I have a distrust of men in general and a negative attitude towards dating. I have not seriously dated anyone in the almost 4 years since my parents officially divorced. I am afraid of relationships after my reluctant involvement in my parents' failed marriage.

Comment

The foregoing account represents what is possibly the most grievous situation for a child of divorce: The parents place the child in the middle. The parents show no strong signs of becoming more civil, logical in behavior, and thoughtful about the well-being of the child—in short, the parents just continue in their anger and acts of hostility. Many young people in our project commented on this worst-case scenario and their feelings of pain about the unresolved nature of their parents' divorce. Their reactions frequently involved mentioning wanting to get away to have a saner life of their own. However, of course, it is difficult to get away from your parents, and most young people need some form of assistance from their parents. Thus, there is a double bind of wanting badly to be free and autonomous in creating one's own world but at the same time wanting the intimacy of a strong family, as well as the practical provisions families can offer.

The final account in this section is by another person "stuck in the middle," a 21-year-old man. He describes the pain of testifying in court at a custody hearing. In the end, however, this commentary foretells a type of qualified hope that is described at length in the next chapter.

This essay will address the topic of children of divorce. I will give an account of my own experiences with the divorce of my parents and intertwine related course materials. I will tell the story chronologically and describe my emotions accordingly.

I was 14 years old when my parents first told us children that they were considering getting a divorce. My sister was 16 and my brother, 9 years old. At first I did not think anything of it because my parents always had a rocky marriage. I can recall many arguments, but somehow things eventually smoothed over. My father often threatened to leave and he did numerous times, but my mother always fixed the situation. However, this time my mother was the one who threatened to leave.

After a couple months my mother made it final that she was getting a divorce. Even up to this point in their marriage, I had seen no difference in their interaction together. This was frustrating to me, because I had absolutely no idea why my mother wanted a divorce. I can remember a few specific instances when I questioned if I might have been a contributing factor in the dissolution of my parents' relationship.

During the early stages of the divorce, I took long walks with my friend Dustin at night and talked about what I felt concerning my parents' situation. He never had much to say, but it helped just to have someone close to me to talk with. Later, I would eventually start talking with my father, who obviously only gave his perspective on the issue. I began to acquire harsh feelings towards my mother. Although I did not confront her about my confusion as to why she divorced my father until years after, I attributed the majority of my frustration to my mother. What would happen next would accentuate my anger towards my mother ten-fold.

My father and we three kids were playing Monopoly on our porch table one Sunday afternoon, when the doorbell rang. Mom answered the door and in stepped two police officers. She had put a restraining order on my father claiming that she, along with us kids, were terrified of him. Mom immediately took my 9-year-old brother Adam to go to the mall so he would not have to endure this despicable scene. For over an hour I helped my father pack up his belongings as he was forced by law out of his own house. Just as he was about to leave, (with no place to go) my mother pulled in the driveway. Adam knew what was happening. He instantaneously broke out in streams of tears, saying that he did not want my father to go.

I would later testify in court, against my mother, on my dad's behalf saying that his children were not at all afraid of him. This was a turning point for me in the course of my parents' divorce. After this despicable performance on my mother's behalf, in combination with being stuck in the middle of arguments, I thought of the situation as their situation, not mine. This view helped me confront my parents about putting me and my siblings in the middle of their problems.

Once I obtained the viewpoint that the divorce was their problem and not mine, I felt an immense pressure lifted from my shoulders. I was still left to deal with the immature attitudes of now bitter rivals, but that was a favorable trade off in my eyes. Years later, I still am often put in the middleman position. I don't mind so much now. I guess I am just used to it. I must say that I no longer have the negative attitude towards my mother. I finally gathered the courage to talk with her about her reasons for the divorce. After hearing her side, I now regret the negative attitude I had towards her for all those years. I hope I will have better communication with my own children to prevent those types of misinterpreted feelings.

DEEP SADNESS

A profound sadness clouds the lives of many children of divorce. It is a sadness that belies their years. They often speak of feeling old and too experienced in the ways of the world. They have seen a lot at an early age. So many of their friends and colleagues in college seem to be having "Leave it to Beaver"-type families, with long, happy marriages being modeled by the parents. For those who have so much pain, however, the model they have seen has left them feeling an abiding sense of loss and pain. The following 23-year-old woman expresses her sadness, which has not abated with time. Her account also reports the frequent issue of an affair as part of the divorce dynamics.

As I was growing up, I was aware of divorce because several of my close friend's parents were getting divorced, but it didn't really become relevant to my life until I was a senior in high school. When my parents first separated and the idea that they might be getting a divorce first came up, I didn't quite know how to react or deal with it, so I took it all in and observed everybody else's reactions and feelings around me. The family I grew up with and had so many memories with was suddenly changing and there was nothing I could do about it, except watch and feel the sadness slowly creep inside of me. I am now a junior in college and that deep sadness has never gone away. Sometimes when I am busy with school and moving on in my life, I am not affected at all by my parents' divorce, but in an instant something will remind of the family we used to be and I get so sad that I can't keep from crying.

One time I came home from school and walk into the house smelling stale cigarette smoke, I instantly knew something was wrong because my dad never smoked inside the house for as long as I was alive and never had I seen a cigarette in my mom's fingers before. I would then find my mom and dad sitting at the kitchen table together, both with a look of such strain and pain in their eyes. I had never seen them look so tired before and I knew that what they must have been talking about was more exhausting than running a marathon. But they couldn't tell me what they were talking about yet, only that they had to work things through. My life felt like a dream because I had to go to school and pretend that everything was as it was before. Home was not so happy anymore. Instead, it was a place I didn't know anymore, filled with tension and sad faces.

After a couple of months of not knowing what was going on, my brother came home from college for Christmas and everything became more clear. A couple of days before Christmas day, my dad told us that he would be leaving soon. I don't remember exactly what he said, because maybe I was trying not to hear what he was saying, so that it wouldn't seem real. But as best as he could, he stumbled out how he had to leave and couldn't really explain why, but that it is something he had to do. I remember how quiet the room was and I could feel in my gut how sad everyone was. But, we still had to decorate the tree and pretend to be happy to celebrate Christmas, knowing that it was probably going to be our last Christmas together. I remember fighting back the tears as I handed my dad the lights to string on the tree while it seemed like every Christmas memory I had with my family went through my head. As for my brother, he was too angry and upset to be in the room and he didn't take part in decorating the tree. He had been away at school the whole time that I saw my parents' relationship slowly deteriorate, so it came as a big blow to him and he was extremely mad and angry at my dad. Then two days later, my dad packed up his things and moved into an extended stay place nearby. Originally, he was just moving out to think things through, but a couple days turned into weeks, weeks into months, until my dad bought his own apartment, and finally his own house. As each day passed, I realized that the chances of him coming back to my mom, my brother, and I were close to none, even though I hoped and prayed that he would change his mind and come back home.

Eventually, we found out the reasons why my dad had to leave, and I realized that my brother had good reasons to be angry, yet I couldn't get past the sadness to be angry with my dad. My dad was the type of person to hold everything inside and he didn't share things with my mom that he should have, which might have saved their marriage. While she thought everything was OK, he was feeling depressed and unhappy with his life. Instead of sharing his feelings with my mom, he found someone else to share them with, resulting in several years of an affair. This made things messy and life became a living hell for my mom. She cried in my arms almost every night for months after their separation, and sometimes even now when I am home from college, I have to comfort her in the middle of the night until she is calmed down enough to fall back asleep. My mom was very small to begin with, but after the divorce, she went down to 90 pounds, maybe even less in weight. So as I would comfort and hold her, I felt like I was the mother and she was the child that I had to protect. During these times of comfort, she would weep and yell out all of the things that she hated about the woman my dad had the affair with, and all of the things that she hated about my father for doing what he did. All of these things were things I didn't want to hear, but I listened because as I watched my mom fall apart, I felt like it was the least that I could do.

Then the day came when it was my turn to go to college and I felt guilty because this time I was the one leaving my mom. This was the time of her life that she thought she would have alone with my dad, where they could travel and enjoy each other without kids. But instead she was left alone, in the house holding all of our families' memories, unsure of how she will be able afford everything, and severely depressed. At the same time that I felt guilty for leaving, I wanted so desperately to begin my new road in life. I wanted to be on my own and learn about the world in a new set of freedoms. I wanted to see how I will grow as a person and what I will experience. And most of all, I wanted to break away from feeling like a child and more like an adult. The only way I could do that was to be away from home, at college, which meant away from my mom as she was going through the most difficult time in her life.

Things have started to change for the better though. We have a cat to keep my mom company, which doesn't take the place of my dad, but he is an excellent cat, the best cat in the world I would have to say, and I don't think my mom could have made it through without him. My mom also got a new job as a secretary of the elementary school that I went to, which she would never have done if my parents were still married. She has the feeling that she can be a little more independent, know how to pay the bills, and take care of things that go wrong in the house, even though those things frustrate her and make her cry and blame my dad for all that goes wrong.

She has a strong circle of family and friends that cheer her up when she is feeling down and keep her busy with dinner, movies, and other activities. But, despite all of these things, I know that she is still hurting and misses my dad, or what they had together, and I don't think that after 25 years of marriage and memories and experiences together, that those feelings will ever go away.

As for how I'm dealing with things, all I can say is that I miss tremendously my dad, how our family was, and the dream of how it would be at this time in my life. I was always close to my dad growing up, and like most girls, my dad was my hero and the person that I looked up to most in my life. Even after what he did, I still love him very much, but our relationship has grown apart which upsets me. Since he left, I haven't been able to talk to him about anything that has true meaning in my life. I haven't even been able to tell him any of my feelings about the divorce because for some odd reason, I don't want to hurt him. Another reason why our relationship is strained right now is because of the fact that there is so little time that we get to see each other. In the beginning, we would only be able to see each other for a couple of hours over dinner in a restaurant. My brother and I weren't comfortable going to his new apartment because it was still too hard to accept that he wasn't with us anymore. And perhaps going there made it seem even more real. So after a year, we finally met my dad at his apartment, but each visit would be a couple of hours and just as we were becoming a little more comfortable with the idea, he bought a house with the lady he had the affair with which brought us back to meeting at restaurants again. Not until this past May, did I visit my dad at the house and have the dreaded meeting with the other woman. It was an extremely tough decision for me to make because I know that I hurt my mom very much by going there. But, I was tired of only seeing my dad for an hour or two at a restaurant, maybe twice a month if I was lucky. I assured my mom that this doesn't mean that I am accepting my dad's girlfriend into my life or want anything to do with her, or that I love my mom any less by going there.

I never thought that I would have to worry about sharing the time with my parents between two houses, but it is something that I have to accept now. I don't like what has happened to our family and sometimes I wish that it was all one long dream, and that I would wake up and find my mom and dad living happily in the same house together again. And in that dream I would wish that my brother and I could go home for Christmas this year and we could celebrate it as a family like we always did. But I can't live life as if it was a dream anymore and I have to accept my parents' divorce as a reality. It doesn't mean that I don't love and miss what we had, nor will I forget any of the memories that we had together. It just means that I have to take life's changes as they are and see what I can make of it. It's a good challenge for me, and will keep me looking for good changes in life that are in my future, rather than more bad ones.

Comment

The foregoing account is remarkable in that the young woman has seen so much pain in her family, yet she ends on a positive note. Like so many children of divorce, it seems clear that she has had to do some of the parenting herself to help her mother adjust to divorce. She also has had to try to keep her anger toward her father in check so that some semblance of a relationship remains for the future.

As John Harvey often mentions to these students in discussing their parents' divorce, they may have many years of interaction with their parents ahead. Most of the students are in their early 20s, and most of the parents are in their 40s. Hence, for the parent with whom no relationship currently exists, there needs to be hope for the future. It is greatly in the interests of the parent and the child to try diligently to resolve hurt so that a relationship is possible for the many years that remain. However, a major challenge for these young people is determining how to do that when there is an abundance of guilt and anger surrounding the divorce.

BECOMING A CYNIC

As has been apparent in these reports, many young people are cynical about relationships after experiencing divorces that were spawned by affairs. The following 20-year-old woman addresses this topic as a central issue. In light of the adverse impacts this woman feels have occurred in her dating life, she might be viewed as a "poster child" for the conclusions Wallerstein et al. (2000b) advanced about the negative effects of divorce on children.

I grew up in a suburban neighborhood in Iowa with my mother and brother. Due to my father's legal troubles and infidelity my parents' marriage dissolved when I was 3 years old. I felt well adjusted to my families living ar-

rangement throughout my childhood. I thought I had it good! Instead of one birthday or Christmas I had two. My father lived with the woman he cheated on my mom with and my mom married and eventually divorced another man. Now at the age of 20 I feel like I may be dealing with issues that could be a direct result of my parents' divorce.

I have been dating a man for 10 months. We do not have a healthy or good relationship by any means. He does not treat me the way I want to be treated, nor does he make time to spend with me. Being a PhD student, he spends a lot of time on schoolwork, but I still feel that if he has feelings for me he could make some time. I do not attempt to communicate my concerns to him for fear that he will be angry with me and want to end things. I tend to have irrational thoughts a lot of the time regarding our relationship. If he doesn't call within a time that is reasonable to me I start to think that he has another girlfriend. Deep down I know that this probably isn't the case considering his lack of time to hang out with me. Another example is when I stay the night at his house, if we wake up and he doesn't have his arms around me or isn't laying right next to me I start to think that he isn't interested in me anymore.

Deep feelings of distrust are constantly on my mind whether it is friends, lovers, or acquaintances. I feel most times that people's intentions towards me aren't good. Or my friends are going to get annoyed with me and not want me around if I hang out too long. It does not take a lot in a friendship for me to feel alienated.

I have seen a pattern to the types of friendships I make and keep. I am very outgoing and can make friends easily. I have a ton of acquaintances and a large size group of people that I would consider good friends. The pattern I see is that, somewhere along the friendship I decide that my friend doesn't like me or seems annoyed with me, in most cases it is a male friend, I then pick a fight with them. I see this as a way of keeping them at an arm's length away. If I instigate a fight, then I have made the first step towards detaching myself from them, and if they are sick of me like I am assuming then it is and was my decision that we shouldn't be friends, not theirs. I feel that I have a good deal of emotional stress due to my lack of trust towards people, and I do see that as a result of my parents' divorce. I think though that there are some positive aspects that came out of my parents' divorce. One of those is my sense of responsibility and caring for others. I had to start caring for myself a lot more after my parents' divorce when my mom had to go back to work. I learned to be independent and get what I needed, from buying my own deodorant and soap to comforting myself when I was sick. I could and still can do it all. I am very empathetic and will drop everything in my life to be with

a friend if they are having a hard time. Sometimes I have a hard time draw-
ing boundaries and go so far out of my way to care for others, such as not
taking care of my own priorities, then I am hurt when they do not do the
same for me. I can although rationalize that they cannot wholly be there for
me if they have other engagements, but it is hard.

I was always told that I didn't need anyone to take care of me, and that
has become the truth. The scary part is that I don't know if I am capable of
letting someone into my life. I don't need anyone to do anything for me, and
relationships call for give and take. The idea that I am so self-reliant makes
me feel like I may have a hard time accepting someone into my world, and
that scares me to death.

I think about my feelings towards relationships a lot and try to be less
guarded, but it is hard. I still deal with the emotional detachment present in
my family, and tell myself that I will just have a family of my own to love.
Then I can right the wrong I have felt. I don't know if the feelings I have are
a result of the life I have due to my parents' divorce or just a result of some-
thing else in my environment, but after reading the Judith Wallerstein book,
I have a sense that my feelings are more valid than I had ever given myself
credit for. It was nice, and sad to read that there are other people who are
dealing with insecurities as numerous and deep as mine.

Similar to the previous narrative, several female students in
Mark Fine's "Process of Divorce" class claimed that they were very
fearful of making a long-term commitment to a romantic partner,
were likely to "test" the fidelity and loyalty of their romantic partner, and lacked trust in men. One 20-year-old woman stated:

When my parents got divorced, I became very disillusioned with romance
and relationships. And, when I found out that my father had been cheating
on my mom, I became even more disillusioned and hated him. Every time I
get in a relationship with a guy, I can't get my dad's cheating out of my
mind—if my dad, supposedly a mature adult, cheated, surely college men
will. I'm always imagining that they are being unfaithful to me and I put
guys through tests that they never can pass (like expecting them to read my
mind and know that I need some comfort or attention, but being afraid to
ask for it directly). I mistrust men so much that I don't know if I can ever
have a healthy long-term relationship with one.

The following account, written by a 22-year-old woman echoes
this cynicism about her ability to successfully navigate her own rela-

tionships. Note her view that her parents have let her down as mentors of effective close relationships.

As I have entered into a stage of my life where I switch from a teenager to a young independent adult, I realize I am faced with more challenges and decisions that I must make on my own. When responding to these challenges I think often of my mentors. My mentors being my parents. However, I realize more and more each day that I want to choose a different path in life than they did. As I look at the two of them in response to what I have learned in psychology on the subject of divorce, it does not make me proud.

Looking at romantic relationships is very different for me. I do not want to follow in my parents' footsteps and end up in divorce. It is a very scary time for me. Not only do I worry that I will want to divorce, I worry even more about putting my all into a marriage and ending up with a husband that doesn't wish to be with me anymore. I am not very secure in relationships. Because I am not romantically confident, this causes many problems. My partner questions why I do things. Why at times I am withdrawn. I feel I do this because I don't want my relationship to end in failure.

Growing up from a divorced family has not only made me second-guess my own relationships but it has affected me in other ways as well. I have become very angry over the past few years upon entering college. My parents have taken on completely different parental roles throughout my life. I am the textbook child of divorce, in a sense that my mom had sole custody of me growing up. I would visit my dad every other weekend and stay with him for a longer period of time during the summer. This all started to occur when I was 7. As I got older the visits to my dad's house slowly dwindled. My father became less and less involved in my life. Because of this I feel I have no male figure in my life to ask for direction. I feel there have been many instances where I should have received disciplinary actions from a father that I never received. Today when my dad tries to tell me I shouldn't or should do something it is very hard for me to listen and obey him. Why should he be able to tell me what to do now when he was never there before?

I try to be patient with him and understand his life. From the age of 9, I received a stepfather, who played a valuable role in my growing up experiences. When I was 16, he passed away. Having a father figure and then not having a father has been a very difficult transition for me. There are times when I am grieving and I think to myself I will never have a real father. One that I know and one that knows ME! It has only been in the past couple of years that I have realized that I still do have a dad. In fact my biological father is still alive! So I struggle today with understanding why he has been such a void in my life. When I get together with my father, it feels as though I am visiting with a man who has been in my life since birth, but is not really my father or someone with authority over me. He seems as though he is someone I was just supposed to know while here in this life. Currently I am working on building a relationship with my dad. I want him to know me, know my future husband, my future family, and my friends. I want him to feel welcome at my house (when I get one).

JUST PLAIN PAIN

The following two excerpts express some of the raw pain that many young people express about divorce in their family. The first was offered by a 21-year-old man and honors student.

I could write ten thousand words on what divorce has meant thus far in my life. I hardly understand the toll on my family's interpersonal relations. Let me just jot down words reflecting my discursive thoughts: numb, sleep, brother, pull tight. My parents have never loved each other. I have never seen them touch. I have never heard them say "I love you." I cannot remember easy laughter or camaraderie with my family; everything has been tension-filled. It has colored my entire personality—my conflict avoidance, my mediation of conflict among friends, my earnest desire to see all points of view, that I border on nihilism now because I have always been able to succeed in school, socially, and everything else that is supposed to matter. But every damn time I get an award, it just hammered home how I could enjoy great success and never contribute to my parents' happiness. This experience with my parents has ruined my own relationship. The end result of my varied thought processes is that I don't know anything about relationships no matter how many classes I take.

Finally, this 21-year-old woman also addresses the deep hurt she has felt in the context of her parents' divorce and how she has tried to run away from that hurt.

My parents got divorced when I was in high school. I remember being a sophomore and joining a divorce support group. For the first time our happy nuclear family was crumbling. My father has never been around much because he owns a business that requires a lot of work, but he also was drinking much of the time.

So I ran away from it all. My friends became my outlet. I avoided my family to stay sane or maybe I just didn't want to know. Things always seem out of control and irrational when it came to my mom and dad. I didn't want to deal with it. My dad promised he would quite drinking, but nothing happened. False promises made me avoid the family even more. My mom began to lose her mind by my senior year. My sister was deep into gangs.

Now, 4 years later, things are better and calmer. New problems have replaced the old ones. I worry about my sister's ability to take care of her 1-year-old baby. I worry about my mom and brother. Each is very vulnerable. I am too. It was "our divorce"—it affected all of us greatly. Divorce is hard. No matter how many details you can say or write, you haven't scratched the surface of your feelings and the extent of loss perceived by so many.

DEATH OF A SIBLING AS A SUBTHEME IN DIVORCE

Although the narratives in this book focus on divorce as the most salient stressor in the students' lives, divorce seldom occurs in the absence of other stressors. Multiple stressors, including those directly stemming from the divorce as well as those that are unrelated, are the norm, not the exception. In this final commentary, the chaos of divorce is coupled with that of sorrow in the loss of a sibling. This 24-year-old woman discusses the shock that hit her when her parents divorced and then the further chaos in her life, because the family's grief was exacerbated by the death of a sibling. The death of a child often places a huge stress on marriages (Harvey, 1996, 2002). This woman, now married and with a child, wonders about how the divorced family she experienced will affect the family she now is developing. This story is unusual because of the role of the death of a sibling in the chain of events.

Divorce as defined by the Webster dictionary is: "a legal dissolution of marriage bond." While this in not an incorrect definition it is not a complete picture of what the word "divorce" really means. It also does not take into account that the word divorce means different things to different people. Following is my definition of what the word divorce is and what it has meant to me and my life.

For the majority of my life divorce was only a concept, a word, to me. My parents were happily married as were the parents of my closest friends. Of those people I did know that were divorced or kids whose parents were di-vorced I had a distant attachment to it. It really meant nothing to me. I had no real understanding of what it meant to be divorced or what it meant to have divorced parents.

In the summer of 1991 I was violently thrown into the "real world." In July of that year my only sibling committed suicide. My parents, as often happens, grieved in different ways. They did not rely on each other and in fact my father turned to another woman for help. Within 6 months of my brother's death my parents had separated and within a year they were di-vorced—after 26 years of marriage.

At the time I was struggling to stay afloat just with the knowledge that my brother was gone. Having my parents divorce was more than I could han-dle. I was unable to attend school (I had just started my first year of college at a community college) and I found it impossible to keep a job. I remained living in the home that I grew up in but it suddenly was a strange house to me. My brother was gone and now my dad was too. To make matters worse my mother started dating and her boyfriend moved in. I hated my mom for this and blamed her for all of these changes. I quickly moved out and lived my father. I wanted nothing to do with my mom who prior to this had been my best friend. Today, I find this interesting as it was my dad turning to an-other woman, having an affair, that ultimately ended the marriage and yet I blamed my mom for everything and I did so for at least a year following the divorce.

My parents both eventually re-married, although my mom has since di-vorced and my dad has had numerous separations from his wife. My par-ents have attempted reconciliation twice—both times discovering that each had changed and grown other ways and they were really no longer compati-ble. Although my parents have remained friends I still hold some resent-ments. Even though my parents divorced when I was an adult (age 19) I still feel that I have lost something. This becomes very clear to me at birth-days and holidays. I resent having to split my time between two people I love and feeling guilty if someone is getting less of my time. Now that I too am married and have a young son it bothers my even more. My son will never experience the kind of childhood that I had always envisioned for him. He too will have to shuttle back and forth between Grandma and Grandpa. I have been told by both of my parents that they would never have divorced if Jim had not died. This only angers me more. I often wonder why they could-n't turn to each other after being together for so long. In my own life I work very hard to ensure that my husband and I don't make those same mistakes. I make a big effort to keep communication open with him.

For me divorce means more than a legal dissolution. It means heartache, change, negative thoughts and feelings, and even insecurities. My story, however, is only one story. Each and every person who has experienced or been around divorce has a different story and a different definition of what the word means to them.

CONCLUSIONS

If the reader had only this chapter as evidence, the evidence would show a lot of resonance with Wallerstein et al.'s (2000b) contentions about the deleterious effects of divorce on children. The themes of despair, chaos, confusion, sadness, cynicism, feeling stuck in the middle, pain, and craziness permeate the foregoing reports. We see in these reports that their parents' divorce often is connected in the minds of young people with other losses they have experienced (e.g., school difficulties, dilemmas with lovers, uncertainty about self-worth). Such connections among stressors amplify the impact of the divorce, particularly when it is a clear reality in the mind of the young person that these sometimes diverse events are interconnected.

This book, however, is not just about loss and perceived chains of loss in the lives of children of divorce. It is also about adjustment and adaptation over time, as well as about gain and hope. Chapter 4 focuses on stories reflecting these positive impacts of divorce.

Children watch their parents' lovers with everything from love to resentment, hoping for some clue about the future.
—(Wallerstein, Lewis, & Blakeslee, 2000a, p. 85)

4

VOICES OF HOPE

I think that I did grow up emotionally faster than a lot of my friends, but I don't necessarily believe this is such a bad quality. I learned to do things on my own and I learned that life does not always go the way that you expect it to go. Having to deal with the unexpected brings character and it makes you see things for what they really are, not just what you see on the surface. So, I can honestly say that I have forgiven both of them and I don't place blame on either one of them.

—22-year-old woman's comments on the positive effects deriving from her parents' divorce

This chapter includes narratives from young people who have experienced less loss and pain associated with their parents' divorces and, as is true with the chapter-opening quote, they have come to different overall conclusions than the authors of the narratives in chapter 3. The respondents in this chapter have observed more "good divorces" (Ahrons, 1994) than bad divorces.

Compared with the students represented in chapter 3, their voices signal more hope and belief in the possibility of coming out of divorce without greatly impaired relationship prospects for themselves. As is true with all of the narrative chapters, however, there is a mixture of pain and loss among these more positive and optimistic storylines.

Table 4.1 presents the major themes of hope reflected in this chapter. They range from students whose parents had relatively "friendly" and civil divorces to those who came to the conclusion that it was better for them that their parents divorced rather than stay in an unhappy ("just good enough") marriage. These themes, and illustrative narratives, are presented in the remaining portions of this chapter are presented in Table 4.1.

FRIENDLY DIVORCE

The first story, from a 21-year old woman, shows how parents can effectively protect their children when the parents divorce.

My parents got divorced when I was 4 years old. They had been married for 7 years. At such a young age I wasn't really traumatized by the experience. One day after preschool, my mom came to pick me up. The back seat was filled with toys and she said to me that today we were going to our new home. To this day my parents have a wonderful relationship. There suppos-

TABLE 4.1
Major Themes of Hope From Students' Narratives

- Divorces can be civil and friendly
- Divorces can lead to better parenting, including that provided by stepfathers
- There are many and varied consequences of divorce, but the net result can be positive for all concerned
- There may be a period of great despair but, with work, a more constructive, hopeful period can follow
- A lot of growth can derive from this time of pain and sorrow
- Parents should not stay in a conflicted marriage simply for the sake of the children

edly wasn't any fighting involved and it has been that way ever since. My dad remarried and I now have 2 half-brothers. My mom dated a few times but is completely satisfied with being independent. She says she might find someone after I get married and settled down. I think men might be somewhat intimidated by her because she [can] do anything a man can do and probably better!!! She has taught me to never fully depend on a man because you never know what might happen. My dad is a doctor, so she was used to having everything in her life.

I myself am adopted which has led to numerous psychological experiences in itself. It used to bother me to think that Catholic Charities trusted my parents to provide a decent home for me and they couldn't even stay together! To become adopted there are a lot of things the future parents must go through to get the baby. Then the truth came out that my dad had been having an affair and he was married 4 months after the divorce. I had never (liked) and still do not like my stepmom but that information increased my dislike. Just a few months ago, I finally did the math of when my brother was born to when my dad got remarried. I knew then why his second marriage took place so quickly. I know it is horrible of me but I almost want to let my brother in on that piece of information.

My stepmom and I have mostly been civil to each other and I have come to realize that she literally "buys" my friendship. When I was younger, each weekend I would come home with at least 2 Barbie dolls and a Cabbage Patch Kid. You could say I've accumulated quite a lot of dolls over the years. Now, we go shopping for clothes, jewelry you name it and that is fine by me.

One positive thing is that I was given 2 brothers whom I love dearly and we get along wonderfully. I love my father like no other.

A 20-year-old woman in Mark Fine's "Process of Divorce" course stated:

Although I was very upset when my parents told me that they were getting a divorce, after a few years I knew that it was for the best. In fact, I couldn't even imagine how my parents had been able to get along as good as they did. After the divorce, my parents really tried to keep me out of the middle. I know that they were angry with each other, particularly my father being mad at my mom, but they always seemed to be able to put aside their differences so that they could do what was best for me. In fact, in the past few years, they have even become sort of like friends again. I don't want to put my kids through a divorce, but, if it has to happen, I hope I can put their needs first like my parents did for me.

Comment

These two stories reflect an overall theme of this chapter: Parents should put the interests of their children high on their list of priorities at the time of divorce. The first narrative is more complicated in that the woman was adopted, and her father had an affair that quickly led to a divorce, remarriage, and the birth of a stepbrother. As we will see throughout the narratives—especially in chapter 6, which focuses on family chaos—complex arrangements among stepfamilies and ex-stepparents or ex-stepsiblings are common and part of the landscape that children of divorce must learn to navigate, and even appreciate, because of the diversity of people and perspectives these arrangements bring into their lives.

In addition, both narratives, especially the second one, illustrate children's ability to both recognize and appreciate cooperation between their parents following their divorce. Parents might find solace in knowing that even though children might not express their appreciation at the time, their efforts to cooperate with each other will pay dividends for their children in the future.

GETTING A "REAL DAD"

Several narratives illustrate the benefits that can be derived from the addition of another supportive adult—a stepparent—into the child's life following divorce. This 22-year-old woman wrote with maturity about a father who chose not to be very much a part of her life and about a stepfather who is well integrated into her life:

My parents divorced when I was 7 years old, and it was the happiest time of my life. Every night in the midst of my parents fighting, I prayed for them to separate. I thought about when Jasmine and Heather spoke about how much they wished their parents didn't divorce. I have always heard of children wanting their parents to rekindle their marriage. This was not the case in my situation.

After the divorce I spent every other weekend with my dad. He only lived down the street from me so our visits were not limited. My mom remarried about a year after the divorce. Then, in fourth grade I moved to Michigan. We still spent time together and I would fly in during the summer and over holidays. In seventh grade I moved to Iowa and our time together began to diminish. I don't know if this was because I was getting older or because we were so far apart. Now, I speak to my father about once a year and I generally think of him as an immature bastard (excuse my language). He has two children 3 years and 6 years old and I love them dearly. I could completely understand Jasmine's feelings when she told us how she tried to be the mature one and make the effort to call her mother. This last Christmas I sent my brother and sister a package with two Iowa teddy bears. I also sent my father a card explaining to him that I would be in New Jersey (where he lives) for the entire summer and telling him how excited I am to see him and my siblings. I have not received a reply from him yet.

One thing that is different from the guest speakers' and myself is my stepdad. I have the best luck in the world; my mom turned around and married a man who would turn into a great father. My stepdad has been my dad for about 11 or 12 years now. I am an only child and he does not have any other children. I am so grateful that my mother divorced my father and married my stepdad. He has [been] a huge part in making me the person I am today. I love and respect him 20 times more than my biological father. He has loved me and treated me has if I was his true daughter.

People say that children of divorce have a hard time in relationships when they grow older; I do agree to some degree. I saw/heard my mother and father fighting night after night. I have grown up to become my mother so everyday I see more of her in myself. I notice during times of conflict in my own relationships how much I blow things out of proportion and say horrible things that I don't mean. This all comes from listening to my parents fight as a child. Despite all of this, I have been lucky enough to see a close to perfect relationship. I see the way my stepdad looks at and acts toward my mom and I know what love is. They do have their moments, as every one does, but I can only wish that my future, long term relationship will amount to my parents.

I look back at the divorce of my parents and I think of it as a very important time in my life. It has helped my to mature and to become more responsible. I have no regrets. I have lost a man who was intended to be my father, but gained a real dad.

In the next commentary a 21-year-old woman shows some of the sophisticated thought and hope that can be readily found in the young as they reflect on their parents' divorces. Her story again reflects the importance that stepparents can play in the lives of children who have experienced divorce.

Coming from a divorced family myself, some of the stories and information presented in class were familiar. Although it seems like the divorces affected their lives more than mine, we are all affected to some degree. Divorce is ever more popular in the Western world as more emphasis is taken away from family and put on personal gain and satisfaction. A lot of friends I grew up with were from a divorced family and as we graduated from high school others became part of a divorced family.

First, a little background on my situation with divorce. My parents were married in 1973 when my mom was 19 and my dad was 23. In 1976 they had my brother and in 1978 they had me. Things went well at first. Problems started to arise when my dad was not emotionally there for my mom and when he was probably drinking more than was wise. My dad failed to be as emotional and comforting over the course of the marriage and about a year before they separated my mom had just lost her dad to cancer and I was born 3 months after that. My mom and dad were separated in the late 1970s and early 1980s, when my mom finalized the divorce so she could marry my stepdad and have my younger brother.

Neither my mom nor my dad was big into drugs. My dad did drink and probably had a problem but was never abusive to my mom or us and always made sure we had the essentials to live. My dad really loved my mom and didn't want the divorce, but agreed so that my mom would be happier. It wasn't a hard divorce for me primarily because I was still too young to know what was going on. My mom did receive child support from my dad and we still keep in close contact with him as he only lives 30 minutes from my mom. He has played a role in my life. I still see him regularly and celebrate all the holidays with him. He helps out with college and has input into my career as an adult. I don't visit him as much as I should, but we are 2 plus hours apart now and both of us have little free time. My dad has since remarried and has two other kids who are 10 and 12 and I have college and my Army career to manage.

At times I do wonder what it would be like if my parents hadn't divorced. Would we be as financially well off as we are now as to where my mom doesn't have to work because my stepdad makes enough? Would I be in college pursuing a degree? Would I have as good as friends as I do now? Would I be as close to my older brother as I am now? Would I be as close to my mom as I am now? Would I party as much as I do now? How would things be different? I don't know.

With my current situation, having lived with my mom and stepdad for as long as I have, I consider my stepdad as my real father also. It is as if I have two dads who have each taught me different things about life. I refer to my stepdad as dad if I was to introduce him to someone and he considers me as if I were his real son. He has always treated me that way and I will always treat him that way. I believe that my stepdad has taught me more about life because of the time we have spent together and all the knowledge he has but I also believe my real dad has taught me things as well in which one wouldn't get unless they had two fathers as I do. One doesn't know how lucky they are to have two fathers until they have to reflect back on their lives and write about it.

Comment

These two narratives speak to the critical role that a stepfather can play in a child's life. The first respondent does not have a continuing relationship with her biological father; the second respondent does. However, each looks to and values their long-term, loving associations with their stepfathers. The second respondent also shows that children are open to having more than two caring adults who play an influential role in their lives, in this case the mother, father, and stepfather.

Each of these respondents also speaks of the maturity that divorce has taught them. The second respondent asks more questions about what might have been if his parents had stayed together. However, each respondent seems resolved that the divorce was best and that the various actors, including themselves, have made good adjustments. The next narrative reinforces this balanced assessment.

PERCEIVING GOOD AND BAD OUTCOMES (BUT MOSTLY GOOD)

Another highly literate account is this 22-year-old man's statement:

Divorce has impacted my life in more ways than one. I disagree with some of the researchers whom we have talked about in class who say that divorce is worse on a child than the parent remaining in the high conflict marriage. I also don't believe that my parents' divorce has ruined my life as some researchers have suggested. I have been impacted in positive as well as nega-

tive ways since the divorce, but I believe that it was the right choice for everyone involved overall.

My parents divorced when I was 8 years old and in second grade. They had a very amicable divorce and still remain friendly today. The fact of divorce itself was hard to accept at first. My parents never really fought in front of me so it kind of came as a surprise. However, I could feel the underlying tension between them and I realized that they spent less time together also. Although it was hard to accept at first because I was a young child, I learned to accept it as part of my life as time went on. They always made sure that I knew that it wasn't my fault and that they both still loved me very much. I got used to the joint custody arrangement of every other weekend and an alternating weekday eventually also. However, once my parents started dating other people, it hit me really hard. I had a hard time accepting the other people in my life. More than anything I didn't want my parents to get remarried at the time because I strongly felt that the other stepparent would try to take my real parent's place.

Eventually both of my parents remarried around the time of my pre-teen and young teenage years. I definitely had a hard time accepting these remarriages, especially my mom's. When I was in seventh grade I had to move to Indiana with my mom because my stepdad had trouble finding a job in Chicago where both my mom and dad lived. I was angry and bitter that I was essentially being taken away from my dad, my friends and my hometown. My relationship with my stepdad struggled for a long time after the move. My real dad and I had always had a close relationship and so the distance between us was extremely hard on both of us and suffered in the long run, as I will talk about later. My dad remarried last although he had dated my stepmom for a many years beforehand. Even though I only saw my dad and stepmom on alternating holidays and for a month each summer, my step-mom and I also had a rocky relationship. Looking back, I was jealous and bitter at my two stepparents for altering the life that I had gotten used to after the divorce.

The main positive aspect that I gained from my stepparents though was my stepsiblings whom I now consider my own brothers and sisters. I was an only child and since it wasn't possible anymore to have biological siblings, stepsiblings were the next best thing. I have four older siblings on my mom's side and two younger siblings on my dad's side now. I love them all very much and have a unique and special relationship with each of them. Another advantage of my parents' divorce and remarriages, besides the gain of family, would be all of the friends and people that I have met. They have each had a strong impact in my life and will remain friends for life. I am *very thankful for their presence in my life. Another positive aspect of the re-marriages is of course my parents' happiness. They are both very happy with their new partners and have each been married for over a decade now. I seri-ously doubt that either one will divorce again, which of course pleases me.*

All around I would have to say that the most negative aspect of the di-vorce and remarriages is the strained relationship between my dad and me. Although we are currently trying to get close again, I am afraid that we will never be as close as we once were before the move to Indiana. I even go to school and live in the same state where he lives now, but I still don't get to see him very often because of both of our busy lives. There are many factors to why this relationship is strained which I won't go into here. I just want it to be known that I love my dad very much and will always hope for our close-ness again someday.

So, even though there is a major negative aspect to the divorce, overall many positive things came of it and I have much better relationships with both stepparents now that I've matured more. I would strongly recommend that parents NOT stay together in a highly conflicting marriage, especially for the children's sake. In the long run I believe that this situation would be more harmful to the children than divorce itself. I have these beliefs from my own experience and from many of those around me that I know, and to me that is more representative than statistics.

A 21-year-old man voiced a similar conclusion:

My parents are divorced. It happened during my junior year in high school. At the time I was shocked. I thought it was my fault, but I then real-ized it wasn't. Instead of letting it take my life over, I used it in a positive way. I grew up much faster and took care of my mother. My parents are still friends today and I've come to realize things happen for a reason. My par-ents were not meant for each other. I have great relationships with both of them, but they are completely different. With my father, I have a father–kid relationship. I let him worry about finances and things of that nature. With my mother, I'm her husband in a way. I take care of the finances and other things like that.

Comment

The authors of these two narratives both agree that the divorce was best and that they have learned to be grateful for the new worlds introduced to them by divorce. Each respondent is committed to making relationships with parents and stepparents work. The first respondent could be a model for how to construe complex situations positively. He wrote with much poise and reflection about the value of having diverse people in his life—people whom he would not know had it not been for the divorce.

The second narrative presents the dilemma of a young man playing a husband-like role with his mother. This account illustrates a common theme in the literature—during the transition after the divorce, and sometimes indefinitely, parents sometimes place their children (usually a daughter, but in this case the son) in the role of confidant. This role may continue until the parent becomes romantically involved with another partner, which can result in the child feeling replaced by the parent's new partner.

In the next story, a 22-year-old woman reasons about the advantages and disadvantages of her parents' divorce and concludes that, given the conflict involved in the marriage, divorce and its aftermath have been better for her and others than if her parents had stayed married. This narrative also shows the variability in adjustment and experiences that can be found in families.

My parents got divorced when I was 8 years old. My older brother B was 14 and I think the divorce affected him much more negatively than it did me, but I will expand on that later. I think that my parents got divorced because they fought so much. For as long as I could remember, they had fought. However, I saw that as mainly being caused by my father's horrible temper, and so I saw it as something that just had to be dealt with. It was a fact of life—they were going to fight and argue and it was no one's fault—simply my father's personality. I really can't remember any fight that seemed to stem from my mother's end. I think that my father was impossible to please, and annoyed at the smallest things. He would get angry for no reason and yell and swear like crazy! He never got physical with my any of us, although at times he would lash out at inanimate objects (e.g., throw a plate against the wall, or punch a hole in a door). I think my mother constantly tried to settle him down and keep a happy home for B and me, but I am sure it was rather difficult to do. I really must stress that my father has the worst temper in the world and this is primarily what I remember from the years that we all lived together. Plus, my parents are extremely different people and rather incompatible I believe. (To be quite honest, I have a hard time picturing them ever being happy together, al-

though they certainly were at first.) My mother is more generous, caring, giving, and selfless than anyone needs to be, while my father is extremely selfish and oftentimes childish. Looking back, I can completely see why my parents divorced, or rather why my mother would want a divorce. The strange thing is, I think it was my father who wanted it, and my mother who suggested counseling and trying to work it out (which obviously did not happen!).

My dad moved out during the summer of 1988. I thought this was pretty strange, although I knew their marriage was not too good. I remember wondering why Dad would want to move away from us. My dad tells me now (and I don't really remember this too well) that I was really upset when he said he was moving. I didn't know where he was going or why he was moving out. He said that I thought he was just going "away" somewhere far away, as if I didn't know where, and that I was worried I would never see him again. Actually he was just moving across town, so this was not the case at all, but apparently I was quite upset about that. My dad has told me that he took me over to his new apartment right away with the first few things he moved. That way I had a tangible place that I knew he would be—it was not as though he was dropping off the face of the earth! He tells me that this seemed to make me feel much better and came home to my mom telling her all about Dad's new place and how cool it was. He says that from then on, I seemed pretty okay with everything.

I remember one thing that bothered me right about the time of the separation. They had not determined for sure that they were going to divorce, and of course they had not really told me what the heck was actually happening, since I was pretty young. I was highly confused about what was going on with my parents. I don't think I had any friends whose parents were divorced so I had no one to really ask. As I said, they didn't tell me too much—all I knew is that daddy was moving out for a "trial separation," whatever that meant! I had heard of this thing called "divorce" that happened to families with parents that didn't get along, and I began to wonder if that was what was going to happen to us. So, one night when my mom was tucking me into bed (my dad had already moved out), I asked her straight up, "Are you and Daddy going to get a divorce? Is that what is going to happen?" And this was the first time I received a straight answer and someone treated me as if I was old enough to deal with what was going to happen. My mom's reply, "Yes, that is probably what will happen in the end. Your dad and I will probably get a divorce." One would think that this would be a devastating blow to an 8-year-old (and it did of course make me sad), but more so I felt relieved to finally have an honest answer and a correct idea of what was ahead for my family. I had been so confused since dad moved out, thinking he might move back and things would be okay. This finally told me that that was probably not going to happen.

I think the fact that I was relatively young when all this happened helped me deal better than my brother. I was at the age where I didn't really question anything my parents did. They were the smart ones, the adults, the authority, and if they made this decision and thought it was the right thing to do, then it must be. I just accepted the divorce as a fact of life, something that had to happen. I trusted my parents' judgement that it was the only way, and I didn't really question that at all. My brother on the other hand, was right at the age where kids seem to question their parents, be embarrassed by them, and think they are "uncool" and have wrong opinions on just about everything. I think he saw what was really going on—that this was a much bigger deal than I realized, and he probably questioned whether it was the right thing. This made it much harder on him. He seemed to come out of the divorce much more effected than I did. He had many problems in high school and my parents both seem to think that it had to do with him not adapting well to live after the divorce. To this day he has much resentment for my dad and I think blames him for the whole ordeal. Actually, now that I am older and can look back at the circumstances from an adult perspective, I feel about the same way!

Ultimately, I am glad that my parents got divorced and that they did so when they did. I was too young to even remember that much about it, and young enough to just accept the fact and not worry much about it. Therefore, I seemed to come out of it pretty much untouched. My brother was not so lucky. I honestly think it has affected him very negatively, with lifelong implications. No doubt he saw much more of the fighting than I did too, so I'm sure it was not just the divorce but rather the years of conflict that affected him. However, I doubt that it would have helped anyone's situation for them to remain married. My dad still has a bad temper, and I don't think that my mother should have to deal with that just for the sake of her children. Our home was much happier and more peaceful after my father left—a much better environment in which to raise children, in my opinion.

I don't mean to sound as though I was not affected at all by my parents' divorce because that is not true at all. However some of the effects I am only beginning to see now. I never realized why this might be, but I have always had a very negative outlook on marriage. I am sure this stems from never having a good model of a happy, healthy marriage. I often doubt that I will ever find someone who is worthy of marrying, simply because I realize how serious marriage is and even if you think that person is right for you, you may found out later that they are totally wrong. If I ever get married I want to be damn sure that it is to the right person and that it will not end in divorce, although I will probably always fear that!

Basically I think the divorce was for the best, although it is extremely unfortunate how people have to get hurt so badly in the process. Incidentally I forgot to mention that my mother was quite depressed and lost a lot of weight after the divorce. It didn't take too terribly long for her to move on and become at peace with it though. I think she knew she had to pull herself together for B and me. The things I really regret are that my mom got so hurt and my dad has not been very helpful in helping to raise us, financially mostly. My mother has had to do an awful lot on her own! I regret that my brother had such a hard time dealing with it, and I think he will never get over the pain and resentment it caused him. I regret that it caused me to have such a negative and pessimistic outlook on marriage and relationships in general. I have a hard time trusting a romantic partner at all, and find it very difficult to let myself feel feelings for a partner. I always try to guard my emotions to avoid getting hurt, and I think I actually miss out on a lot of happiness in the process.

I am glad that I did not have to live most of my life in a house full of conflict. What I remember is bad enough and I can't imagine having to deal with that on top of everything an adolescent goes through. I was lucky to have the most wonderful mother to help me in every way—she has made my life happy and done everything in the world for me! This brings me to another good point I took from the divorce—my closeness with my mom. After Dad left, B, Mom, and I became very close. Then B moved out when I was 12 so I had about 7 years where it was just my mom and me. We developed an extremely close bond—she is my very best friend. She has been amazing to me and I think that I have been a friend to her, even when I was younger! I have much respect for everything she has done and all she has come through.

My relationship with my father used to be pretty good. I viewed him as more of a friend than a father figure I think. I used to spend every other weekend with him until high school, and we would have a good time more or less. When I started not liking him as much was when I was old enough to see his flaws, the mistakes he has made, and his blame in the whole situation. He could have been much more of a father to both B and me, but I guess that is just life. I do hope that someday I might get past much of the resentment I have only recently started to have towards him, and that maybe someday he could realize how he has not been the ideal father at all.

This report has forced me to realize many emotions I have in regard to my parents' divorce! I thought this would be very short and that I had little to say, but when I got started thinking about it I realized all sorts of things that I wanted to say. There is more, but many of my emotions I do not even know how to articulate! One thing I really want to say is that although divorce is a bad thing, and hurts everyone in the process, it can be the best answer sometimes. Children can go on and have a perfectly normal life. I consider myself to be a well-adjusted person for the most part, who is headed on the right track, and who has had a pretty happy life overall. I certainly don't think I would be better off had my parents stayed married! Divorce can also bring about positive things, like a much closer more meaningful relationship with one (or both) parents (many of my friends with married parents are jealous of my close relationship with my mom), and a maturity that is hard to learn without being forced in this manor. My parents' divorce was a nasty thing for everyone involved, but we have all moved on more or less and learned some life lessons in the process.

Comment

The preceding account summarizes many of the key points about why children can adjust successfully to divorce and its consequences. It is important that this woman feels that the marriage was much too conflict ridden to continue and that it was best that she did not have to endure many years of fighting between her parents. She believes that her brother has not adjusted as well to the divorce. She indicates that he was in the middle of the conflict and was old enough and aware enough that he knew what was happening, and he may have been asked to take sides in the conflict as well. This commentary illustrates how important it is to take the child's age and developmental level into account when trying to understand reactions to and consequences stemming from divorce.

COMING THROUGH THE WILDERNESS AND FINDING HOPE

Many of the young people's stories in this book speak volumes about the devastating consequences associated with ugly or ill-timed divorces. However, many others feel that they have developed strength and maturity. Many young people feel quite devastated by ugly divorces and vow to avoid such developments in their relationships. This account from a 21-year-old woman is illustrative:

Divorce is such a commonality—especially in the U.S. anymore. It is reported that 51% of the people in this country have been divorced. I think people really need to take that statistic into account and realize that marriage is not something you just jump into or do for fun. Marriage, like anything else will have its negatives. And I feel that people need to be aware of that before they do anything pertaining to marriage. It just seems to me that people are not wanting to assume marital responsibility anymore and the only way to get out of that responsibility is by getting a divorce.

First, I will give you a little of my maternal family history concerning divorces. My grandmother and grandfather were married before they married each other. They were both at age 18 when they got married to their previous spouses. My aunt, my mother's sister, was married 10 years when her husband decided to leave her for another woman. And my mother got married 23 years ago to my biological father. She gave birth to me a year after they were married. He, not being ready to faithfully be a husband or a father, decided to leave my mother when I was 6 months old. With the divorce, he took everything—even jewelry and a car that was my mother's. My mother had lost almost all the things she owned—except her clothes, the house, and yours truly. As a matter of fact, he wanted nothing to do with me after they divorced, which didn't affect me too much because I did not know the man anyway. But, my mother was another story. Not only did she lose many of her personal belongings, but she lost her partner and a man she loved very much. She was ready for the marriage, but he was not.

Thankfully, a year or so later, my mother started dating my "dad," and he has been my dad ever since. My parents got married when I was 5 years old and 6 months later my brother was born. You're probably thinking, "Hmm, that's a pretty happy ending ..." but to be honest with you, it is a little more complicated than that. My mom had lost her first husband, so it took her 5 years for her to gain the courage back to trust another man in matrimony. I remember there were nights when my dad would be gone at work on the midnight shift when I was a small child, and my mother had just had a nightmare. I could just tell by the look on her face and by the words she said that it was about my father. I would just hug and hold her till she stopped crying.

Since divorce runs in my family like water through a hose, I hope to be the one to break that chain when/if I ever do get married. I look at the marriage

my mom and dad have, and all in all, it is a good one. Through their argu-
ments and disputes, they've managed to be married for 16 years.

I've witnessed some pretty ugly conflict, but they endured the hardships
and have done the best job they could. I really take pride in that because
you don't see that too often anymore. I agree with Wallerstein's idea that
people should stay married to an extent to which people should work on
their marriage as best they can and really know each other before they are
ever married and before they plunge into something they possibly will not
be able to handle. The difference between my views and Wallerstein's views
is that she is much more opinionated than I am concerning divorce be-
cause she believes that more or less that divorce should not even exist. I, on
the other hand, am not quite that adamant in my beliefs. To be honest, I'm
tired of viewing marriages as delicate when they should be rock solid. The
vows of "till death to us part" should be taken into account, and I think
that was what Wallerstein was really trying to say. In conclusion, I feel
that marriage is not something to be taken for granted or dealt with as a
game. Marriage is a lifelong commitment. And until people start believ-
ing that, the U.S. will probably continue to climb the trend of divorce. I feel
that doing all that is possible to save marriages is what needs to be done,
and divorce should only be considered as a last resort.

Another 21-year-old woman also revealed strength after enduring much loss associated with her parents' divorce:

Divorce is a very hard concept, something that affects everyone in-
volved. I myself am a victim of divorce. My parents divorced when I was
13, probably the most crucial time in my life. I was experiencing so many
new things, starting a new school (middle school) making new friends, go-
ing through puberty, and I was also diagnosed with diabetes that same
year. I helplessly felt that my life was falling apart. Two years previous to
my parents' divorce, my father had an affair with another lady, one of my
mother's friends actually, who my father worked with. My parents tried to
work it out, they seemed to be happier than I ever remembered following
that. However, my mother then found my father and the lady he was hav-
ing an affair with together again a year and a half later. That is when they
decided to call it quits.

Divorce has changed my life. My siblings and I moved with my mother.
Thankfully my parents still got along well enough that they mutually
agreed that when my father wanted to see us he could, there were no strict reg-
ulations as to child custody. I missed our family all being together. My older

brother and sister were in high school and were never home at all it seemed like, probably because they felt that it was not really home without all of us together. Dinnertime was always when my family would sit down together and talk about each other's day and just reminisce , we no longer had that, we did, but it was only my mother, little sister and me usually. Being from a small town, everyone knew everything that was going on with my family, I was so embarrassed I remember.

Out of all of my friends, I was now the only one whose parents were divorced. When I would go to my friends' houses and see a happy family bonding, I would hurt, long for that once again. Everyone was so supportive though, thank God. My mother and I formed a very close bond, she became my best friend, she needed me, and I needed her. I was also still very close to my father and continue to be today. I was always Daddy's little girl, and when he did this to my family it was so hard for me to understand it. Fortunately I am a very forgiving person, and decided I needed to put the past behind me, and rather live for today and the future.

I have struggled throughout life since the divorce, but it has only made me a better, stronger person. I have learned responsibility, learned how to be a hard worker (I have had a job since I was 14 and am now putting myself through college!) I am a very grateful person, I am content and very happy-go-lucky. I realize that divorce was the best thing for my family right now. I often wonder what it would have been like if my parents would not have gotten divorced, but then think to myself, everything happens for a reason, and I am who I am today because of what has happened to me in the past, and made me that much more of a better person!

Comment

As is evident from these stories, young people have to work hard to find positive aspects of the trying circumstances of their parents' divorce. The first respondent provided a classic line in this collection of narratives when she wrote "*Since divorce runs in my family like water through a hose,*" reflecting the intergenerational (and intragenerational) transmission of divorce noted in chapter 1. Still, both writers show perspective and strength in meeting these challenges and believing that they can handle other events that no doubt will be part of their long-term adjustment to divorce in their family.

A final "wilderness to hope" story is provided by the following narrative, written by a 21-year-old man who muses about how divorce at any point in a child's life can be devastating. But then the person has to get up off the ground and go on and, after surviving, the person may see that the long-range outcome is better than if the divorce had not occurred.

Divorce is a very traumatic event—it's difficult for everyone involved. Each family member is impacted, whether it is the parents or the children. I often wonder what the best age is for a child to experience divorce. Would it be easier for a 6-year-old, a 16-year-old, or a 26-year-old? I guess it depends on the circumstances, but I think that it would have been hardest for me as a teenager. Going through my parents' divorce was very difficult for me, and I was away at college 90 percent of the time. I could not imagine what it would have been like if I still was living at home.

When my parents announced that they were going to get a divorce, I felt that my parents owed it to me and my brothers to stay together no matter what. I was not going to allow it to happen. I remember everything about that day; what went on, where I was; my initial reactions. I had just finished my freshman year of college, and returned home for the summer. My parents gathered us around the kitchen table, and told us that their relationship was over. The conversation began with my father saying, "Your mother and I have something very important to talk to you guys about. What I am about to tell you has been the most difficult decision that we have ever had to make ... " At that exact moment, I knew what they were going to say. After my parents finished telling us what they needed to tell us, I became extremely upset, claiming that this was not going to happen. I didn't care what it took, divorce was not an option. I felt it was the easy way out, and the effects would be too severe.

Basically all of my close relationships changed following my parents' divorce. The relationship that I have with my brothers and father is stronger than it has ever been. The relationship that I have with my mother and girlfriend (now ex-girlfriend) has weakened. It was amazing to me how different my views on life and relationships have changed because of the divorce. I think that I am a very different person now, and see the world in a different way.

Recovery is an important part of the grieving process and I feel recovered. Life has its ups and downs, but I truly believe that everything happens for a reason. For some unknown reason, I was supposed to experience divorce; maybe it was to strengthen who I was; maybe it was to open my eyes regarding relationships; maybe it was to bring me closer to my brothers; maybe it was to forever change the relationship that I have with my dad. When I say that I am recovered from my parents' divorce; this does not mean that I am "over" my parents' divorce. I don't think that I will ever be "over" it. How could I get over it? It was a traumatic event of my adolescence, and it permanently altered who I am. Life does go on, however, and I am continuing to play the cards that were dealt to me. I am a different person now compared to when my parents were still together, but I would like to think that it is for the better. I have grown a lot from my experience with divorce, and I think that I am a stronger person because of it.

IN THE END: GROWTH AND HOPE

The following 22-year-old man addresses a common theme: If one can survive this loss and the surrounding tumultuous events, one can grow in ways that otherwise would not have been possible this early in life.

Before the beginning of my sophomore year in college my parents got a divorce after being married for 27 years. This came as a shock to me, because my parents had always seemed so happy around each other prior to me leaving for college the year before. One of the major reasons for the divorce is that my parents got married when my Mom was 18 and my Dad was 19. They were fresh out of high school and thought that getting married was the best option for both of them at that time. Ten months after being married they had their first child, which was my older brother Aaron. Having a child so early in the relationship never really gave them the opportunity to develop their own personal relationship with one another. This would cause problems down the road when I, being the youngest, graduated from high school and moved out of the house and on to college.

My mom was the one who initially told me that they were having problems and they were going to marriage counseling to try to start a relationship with each other that they never really had for the 27 years that they were together. With all the kids being gone nothing was theirs in their own relationship. My dad never even talked about my parents having problems until the divorce was almost final. I think it was hard for him to tell his son that Dad had made mistakes in his own relationship and now I was going to have to pay the consequences of those mistakes.

I often found myself getting mad at my mom because I thought she was not putting the same effort toward getting back together as my dad was. My dad often would make me feel guilty because he felt lonely being home by himself. This put an added strain on my own life while I was trying to balance *school, work, and the fact that my parents were never going to be together again. Although my parents and friends were still always there for me, I still cried and thought at night why is this happening to me?*

My anger seemed to be towards my mom more so than my dad because I had feelings that my mom was not telling me everything and that maybe she had even cheated on my dad with another man. I don't really know why I had these thoughts, but I think it was due to the fact that my mom seemed to move on and not let it bother her, while my dad was telling me he still loved her.

Many other things developed from the falling out of the relationship that I probably would have never have known if they had not of gotten a divorce. A year before I was born my dad's mom died. Growing up I was just always told that she got sick and died, but what had really happened was that she committed suicide and blamed my mom for making her do it. She blamed my mom because she said that she took my dad away from her and the only that she could get my mom back for doing it was by committing suicide. Although my dad knew that she was sick and was not thinking clearly he subconsciously always had held this against my mom, making the relationship so hard to make work after the kids were gone.

Although the divorce was very painful for me I also learned a lot about relationships and what it takes to make them work. One of the most important things I learned was communicate with one another. You need to confront the problems when they occur, not years down the road. You also need to develop a strong relationship with your partner before you start to have kids to ensure a successful relationship after they have left the house. My parents were always good to each other when they were around us kids and I am very thankful for that. I never knew until I got to college that my parents were having any type of marital problems at home. It came as a great shock to all of our family and friends. I have forgiven my mom and dad and know that they both love me unconditionally and that is all that really matters. They are both great parents and we all make mistakes we must learn from those mistakes however and move on with our own lives. My relationship with my entire family has become stronger since the divorce of my parents and my appreciation and love for them has grown stronger. I guess things do work out for the best.

Comment

This narrative points to the learning that a child of divorce may acquire when he or she is involved (at least to some extent) in parents' divorcing process. It also shows how reflective young people can be in later understanding the sources of their earlier anger and frustration, in this case his anger at his mother for seemingly not working as hard at repairing the marriage. In addition, this man discusses factors that he learned in watching his parents divorce that he believes are essential to making a relationship work. He also has seen how death (the suicide of his grandmother) entered the picture in terms of having a great impact on his father. His conclusion about the strength of his current family relationships gives hope to other young people that they can survive and learn in the midst of their pain.

A similar theme of growth is sounded by this 22-year-old male. In his well-written story, he stresses the added responsibility that often devolves to the older children of divorce. He also took the interesting step of interviewing his parents to try to understand better why their divorced happened.

It was a Saturday morning in late May back in 1988, I was in fourth grade. Mom and Dad were sitting on separate sides of the room: symbolic of the paths their lives were taking. I knew the words even before they came out of Dad's mouth, but they hurt nonetheless. He said that Mommy is going to start living somewhere else, and those words pierced me like a knife; I ran to my room crying. I don't know what made me so upset, but I cried all day. I took it very personally that Mom and Dad were getting divorced. I think that I felt sorry for myself, I didn't want to be one of "those kids" with divorced parents. All the kids I knew with divorced parents were stuck in day care and always had messed up family lives—there were just so many negative connotations associated with divorced families.

In the following days I didn't know how to act. I was sad and felt like my life had been changed for the worse and would never get better. I also had the feeling that all of a sudden I would now have to raise myself—which I never really got over. In the weeks following the divorce I noticed that both parents had lost a lot of weight, and Mom had a terrible cold. I could see Dad was very stressed out, because now he was responsible to not only managing a business but also managing a household.

In studying divorce and dissolution, it is apparent that traumatic events in a couple's life have a profound effect on their relationship, and many times lead to divorce. My mom dealt with depression and alcoholism for many years, and she attempted suicide 2 years prior to my parents divorcing. Looking back I am not surprised my parents divorced, after all, the mental stress on them both was significant. It was initially very hard to cope with their divorce and I took it very personal, which led to years of bitterness. As the years went by after the divorce, the emotional trauma still lingered and I never felt like I was very close with my parents. The responsibilities required of me living in the household of a single parent were a tough initial adjustment, but I feel I am a much better person because of it. I feel a sense of accomplishment and confidence in working to keep our household functioning for so many years. I also have been able to pinpoint one of my personality traits: the feeling that I should always be pleasing people. For most of my teen years my mom would get upset when I wouldn't meet her emotional needs; so I worked to counter that by always trying to please her and make her happy in order to prevent her from being upset, which always stressed me out.

Recently my dad has remarried, and it has been a very happy time for all of us. The fact that he is in a stable, loving relationship is just a huge ease to my mind. The weeks after the wedding I noticed a difference in my psyche. I really felt a lot of closure on my parents' divorce. I had never realized the weight my subconscious feelings about the divorce had on my overall mental health.

Coming to college was a very positive experience for me. It gave me some perspective on the family I have come from, a family I love very much; but for my own mental health, I needed some distance from them. There is a lot of significance in my parents remarrying—those events have brought closure on my lingering feelings of loss from the divorce. It is true that writing is a great way to cope with a loss, but I also feel that more importantly, writing is a way to better understand the loss.

There was one topic in my life that I did not have answers to. I have not had answers in 15 years. I do not have the answers, and I know who does. However, this topic is not talked about in the detail that it needs to be in my family. It is brushed aside as something that is in our lives, but we are not going to think, share, talk about it. You can't change what happened, so why cry over spilled milk? Well, this was not good enough for me. How come I do not know these answers? I am part of the family. I should know and understand why my parents got a divorce.

Biting my lips and gritting my teeth, I decided that I had to interview my brother, my sister, my mom, and hardest of all, my dad. Yes, I had to do this. What? What was I thinking? I can't do this. See, my parents were divorced when I was 7 years old. Why they were divorced? I have the same answer as you do; I don't know. Can you believe it? Sure we have adapted divorce into our family, but why was there one in the first place? After all these years, I don't know. It was something that was not talked about. Not the right way to go about it. To put things more in perspective let's just say that I had no clue when my parents were even married. We are talking about the day, the month, the year. Frustrating.

So, I figured I would almost use this course writing assignment as a scapegoat in order to do a little investigating to find the answers to my questions to gain some understanding (thank you). I figured if I do not know by the age of 22, when am I going to? What I did was make up a series of questions for my brother and sister, and I filled those out as well for the full effect from the children. I did not want only my view on this since by no means do we all have the same emotions on the topic. Then I wrote out the part that made me almost a little nervous. Who was I to ask my parents these questions, I thought? Well, why not I told myself; no one else has. This is the time to do it.

I had no idea about the emotional divorce part of my parents prior to these interviews. I have learned in "Psychology of Interpersonal Relations" from Professor John Harvey that typically in a marital relationship, one of the partners thinks about divorce for an average of 6 years before actually finalizing it. It became apparent to me what my dad was thinking before the mention of the word, divorce. It was bizarre to me that my parents had different dates for the initial discussion of divorce and also when it was finalized.

I feel this awkward sense of relief. It is almost strange to me, though, because when I interviewed my mom, the conversation was 76 minutes long. I cried immensely. There was also a heated argument, initiated with my spark. I was not satisfied with how she accepted the divorce (if I can even say that). There are mixed feelings about it. On the complete opposite end of spectrum, I came away a lot better off than I thought with my dad's interview. I was shocked with a few answers, but I liked his advice in regards to waiting for marriage with valid reasoning. My mom did not want to "go down that road" when I asked her to do the interview. I do feel better though that I told her and expressed to her what I have felt for these 15 years without answers. My dad told me in the interview that he has not talked about this at all. He does not share his emotions like that. I felt that it was good for both him and me to hear his responses.

I have also talked to my brother and sister about this. They were shocked to hear that dates didn't even match up. Erika wants a copy of this, and Joe wants to hear all of our mom and dad's answers.

In a weird way I feel better about this. I asked the questions, and I got the answers. Some surprised me to this day. I like the fact that this issue was ad-

dressed and was not brushed aside this time. I feel like there is closure on the divorce now.

Comment

We learn from the preceding story that asking parents to tell about their divorce can be an emotionally draining step but also a greatly healing step for the young adult. This interview helped him not only understand their positions but also vent some of his feelings. It also helped his siblings know that it was a useful step to try to understand. Now they also are curious to know more. Did the interview also help his parents? We do not know, but one could surmise that it might have been a positive step for them in being more open with their children about their feelings regarding the divorce.

WILL NOT ACCEPT "JUST GOOD ENOUGH"

Several young people took issue with Wallerstein, Lewis, and Blakeslee's (2000b) argument that implied the importance of staying with the "just good enough" marriage. The following stories exemplify reservations regarding such logic. The first was written by a 21-year-old woman:

My parents divorced when I was 5 years old and I lived with my mom for a few years before moving in with my dad. I really don't remember anything about their divorce except for the one time when I was really little that I could hear them shouting at each other in the kitchen. I remember being scared and wishing they would stop.

My dad started dating J when I was 8 years old, and she helped him to raise my sister and me. They were married in 1994 and she has always been like my own mom. Living with her and my dad all through junior high and high school influenced the person that I am today.

It was a complete and total shock to me when Dad and J announced that they were divorcing in my senior year of high school. I saw no signs of this coming and felt like a sledgehammer had hit me in the chest. It seemed to me that their marriage was the one stable thing I could count on and suddenly it ceased to exist. I knew I would still see J often and we would continue to be friends, but the relationship would be forever changed after their divorce.

Although their divorce would alter my views of marriage, I cannot say that I agree with Wallerstein's opinions on divorce. She seems to base her theories on the assumption that divorce is terrible for kids and it's an experience that they will never get over regardless of their future relationships with others. I find this assumption troubling because although their divorce changed me, I think it was for the better because it made me stronger.

I admit that I do look upon the institution of marriage with a wary eye. I think that is a normal reaction for any person to have, especially a young woman in her 20s. I still want to have kids some day and I know that one day I will probably be married also. I don't think that their divorce changed my views on that. I also think that staying in a marriage that is "good enough" is a waste of the lives of everyone involved. Why stay in a situation where both people are unhappy and do not love each other? To say that it is in the best interest of the child is ridiculous. You can only shelter a child for so long before something traumatic happens—it's a part of the growing process of life. More important than staying married is for both parents to continue to be there for the child and to keep the relationships strong.

I see J every weekend when I go home, and we are still best friends. I respect that Dad and J did what they had to in order to be happy, and I am grateful that they love me and my siblings enough to do what is best for our family. I couldn't ask for anything healthier.

Comment

The foregoing narrative makes points similar to one that we both have heard from many young people about the idea of parents staying together for the kids' sake—even if the marriage is horrible to barely tolerable. "Don't do it!" is the message these students scream out in unison. In so doing they are endorsing the idea that parents deserve to be happy in their intimate lives. They usually also are implying that their parents' happiness contributes to their own happiness.

Next, a 21-year-old woman also reflects on her differences with the Wallerstein et al.'s (2000b) position:

I am 21 years old and my parents got divorced a year ago in February. All throughout my childhood I remember my parents fighting verbally with each other. It seemed like there was never a "peaceful dinner" or family time with my family. My brother hardly talked while he grew up and he sometimes got scared when my parents would blow up in anger at each other. I remember that most of their arguments seemed to be about petty little things that really shouldn't cause so much distress. I learned to live with the arguing, but it did affect me in different ways.

For instance I was embarrassed to bring friends home because I was afraid that my parents would get into a fight and my friends would feel uncomfortable. Also, I couldn't talk to my mother or father when I needed to because they were usually busy arguing. It also affected my brother. He also feared bringing friends home and his school performance was poor. Was this because my parents spent less time helping him with schoolwork and more time fighting?

I disagree with Judith Wallerstein's theory of "just good-enough marriages." Wallerstein says that if a marriage is "just good enough" that the couple should stay together because it benefits the children of the marriage. In my case that is not what should have happened. My parents did have a "just good-enough" marriage—they weren't abusive or physically fighting or yelling at my brother and I (except for once in awhile). This "just good-enough" marriage, however, did not benefit my brother and me. I can't help but wonder how different my life would be if my parents had divorced sooner and had relieved my brother and me from the constant verbal fighting. Perhaps my brother would have spoken more because the fighting that prohibited him from doing so would have been gone. Perhaps I might have a closer relationship with my father because he would have had more time to focus on our relationship without having to spend most of the time arguing with my mother. My brother might have done better in school. I don't know how I would have turned out if my parents had divorced sooner, but it would be interesting to find out.

Even though my parents did not divorce until recently, I somehow always expected that they would someday divorce. I always hoped that they wouldn't divorce, because I knew kids at school with divorced parents and knew how other kids perceived them. I didn't want kids at school to think that way about me. I wanted to have a "whole" family with no problems. I dealt with "knowing" my parents were probably going to get a divorce by looking into the future to see what it might be like for me. Luckily, I didn't have to "deal" with my parents' divorce until I was on my own and in college. It was still difficult to deal with, even though I mostly saw it as a "good" thing because they would no longer be fighting. I also hoped that the divorce would bring them closer together and maybe make them more like friends, because that is what I heard sometimes happened in divorces. It was not like that though. My parents still fight like they used to whenever they are together. They still *have to communicate and be together sometimes because of my brother and me. Another result of the divorce is my feelings about my parents. My largest and most frequently occurring feeling is the feeling of fear. Fear that my parents will not manage alone, fear that my parents will be alone for the rest of their lives, fear for my parents' loneliness, fear that I might loose touch with my father, since we have never been that close.*

I feel responsibility as well. I feel responsible for maintaining contact with my father, because if I don't, he might not make the effort. So far, I have been proven wrong and my father calls me often and e-mails me. I also feel responsible for making sure my parents are doing OK. I "check up" on them often by calling and asking how they are. My brother doesn't do much of anything like this. He also views the divorce as "good," but he seems not to make any effort whatsoever in maintaining contact with my father (they haven't had a great relationship either). He just waits for my father to call. He also verbally fights with my mother sometimes and doesn't seem to consider her feelings when he says awful things to her. Is this a result of being exposed to my parents' harsh arguments for all those years? I, on the other hand, have a very good relationship with my mother and very rarely argue with her. I am also very aware of my mother's and father's feelings and want to make sure that they never feel lonely. My brother just comes and goes as he pleases, and never thinks about how worried my mother might feel if he doesn't come home (he lives at home with my mother).

I know there are no concrete answers to the questions I have posed in this short essay, but I still wonder whether it would have been better if my parents would have gotten divorced sooner and stopped the negative environment my brother and I lived in, or if it was better that they got divorced when they did.

Comment

We see in the preceding story a young woman who believes that divorce was necessary in her family. She even believes that her brother and she would have been better off if the divorce had occurred sooner. Note how much responsibility she assumes for her parents' not feeling lonely and for her brother's welfare. She shows a common profile of maturity beyond her time, a development that no doubt at least partially evolved from the divorce and its consequences.

A NUANCED POSITION

The following 20-year-old woman reveals the nuances in conclusions about the benefits and drawbacks of divorce that young people feel in evaluating their situation and Wallerstein et al.'s (2000b) thesis:

"Unlike the decision to marry, the decision to divorce rarely occurs by mutual consent in families with children ... one partner wants to get out of the marriage with a great deal more passion than the other ... one may not want to get out at all." This quote, from Judith Wallerstein's Surviving the Breakup, *describes what happened when my parents divorced. I am a child of not one, but two divorces. Many people find my family to be abnormal, which it is. I have four parents, two half brothers and one full sister. I am very comfortable with my family situation, but I wasn't always.*

My real mother and father got married soon after college but divorced when I was not even 2 years old. This divorce is not the one I will be talking about in this paper. My mother remarried when I was 3 years old. My stepfather, Tom, was my ultimate father figure. I did see my real dad but I didn't live with him so Tom was more of a real guardian than him. Growing up with my mom and Tom seemed normal to me. Our family wasn't different than anyone else's, I just had bonus parents—I would spend most of the time with my mom and Tom and then every other weekend with my dad and his new wife—Sheila. At first I didn't like to go to my dad's; in fact I would ask my mom who the strange man was whose house we always went to! As I grew older I enjoyed going to my dad's—he would give us sugar cereal and take us to movies—things we didn't always get to do at home. Back at home we had more rules. We could only play with friends once a weekend, we had bedtimes, and my mom was a nutrition freak so I never ate sweets. Tom was the one who laid down the rules—for this I would often get angry with him and go crying to my mom. But my mom would do nothing. She actually enjoyed having a disciplinary figure because she felt she couldn't do it.

But as time went by and I grew older, I realized that my mom was never happy. She and Tom were always arguing—and I mean always. I never thought what would happen would—but one day it did. I remember my mom and [my brother] Paul saying that we were going to have a family meeting. We all sat down and before I knew it Tom was crying. I couldn't stand to see a grown man cry. I was in 7th grade—I knew what they were about to tell us. Tom said through tears, "your mom and I are going to sep-

arate." I started to bawl and I wouldn't talk. I was so angry. My mom wasn't crying, but Tom was. What was going on? Why was my mom doing this to Tom I kept thinking. Soon after Tom moved out into a tiny apartment. I felt so badly for him—I hated my mom.

There is so much else I would like to tell about this story but I can't possibly do it in a few pages. I am now 20 years old and a whole lot has changed. My mom is dating someone else and is finally happy—and I am happy for her. It took me a long time but I understand why she divorced Tom and I accept it. She was not happy and everyone deserves to be happy. I did go through some rough times after the divorce. I had constant feelings of guilt, like there was something I could do to help the situation. I also was very angry. I distanced myself from my family and lost a sense of identity in high school. It took me until sophomore year of college to really work through a lot of issues about the divorce and the aftermath of it.

I don't like divorce. I really think people are getting married without thinking long and hard about what "marriage" means. I think people don't take marriage seriously, and it is causing many unnecessary divorces. I don't want to make the same mistakes my parents did but I don't hold them at fault for what they did. I feel that if a married couple is having problems they should try their hardest to work them out, especially if they have children. But if problems cannot be worked out, the couple should not stay together, even for the children. I know what it is like to live with parents who are constantly fighting and I am so much happier to see my parents happy today, even though apart. I don't plan on marrying until I am positive I am ready and compatible—but even then I guess you never know.

Comment

This account "tells it like it is" for so many children of divorce: This woman hardly likes divorce. She will not get married unless she feels strongly that her marriage will survive. She believes in trying to work out problems. But she also does not believe that highly conflicted marriages should be preserved, even if there is an argument that such marriages are better for kids than are divorces. Also, she is pleased that her mother is finally experiencing the happiness that everyone deserves to have.

In the following, final story, nuances and sophisticated thought are revealed again by a 21-year-old man who believes that there are major benefits deriving from his parents' divorce and that the pieces may have fit together in the long run of this divorce. He also discusses an idea common to children of divorce, that he does not want to put his kids through this process someday. Note a common aspect of many of these narratives throughout the book: vivid, abiding memories of the feelings of sadness and loss the first time the child hears of the divorce.

I believe it would be fair to say that going through a divorce is one of the most difficult things a child could go through. Divorce impacts the life of a child in so many unimaginable ways. Not only does it affect the family structure in general, but it also has a tremendous impact on the social life and self-esteem of the child who is going through the divorce.

My parents went through a divorce when I was in the first grade. At the time, I did not feel the direct impact of the situation, but soon [found] out it would change my life forever. My parents sat us down. I still remember it like yesterday; my brother and are were playing in our "playroom," and we got a call from our parents to come out into the living room. They were each sitting on one end of our maroon couch, and told us to sit down between them. Even at my young age, I knew that something was not right. Little did I know that soon I was going to realize that I was not going to grow up in the typical American family that most of my friends and family were accustomed to.

Both of them looked at us with fear and sadness in their eyes, for they knew the news was not going to make us happy. They explained to us how much they loved us, and both began to cry as they told us that they were going to live apart, Dad was going to move out, and my brother and I were going to live at home with Mom. This is one of the two times I have ever seen my father cry, not because he was sad about the divorce necessarily, but because he was not going to be living with his children anymore. Ben and I first thought that we were the reason that they were getting the divorce, but they explained that it was for the better and we were not the reason that the divorce was happening.

Today I can now look back and be happy about my parents' divorce, and realize it was for the better, but the happiness that I have today definitely came at a high cost. The divorce up to this point in my life is the hardest thing I have ever had to go through. I think that only the death of my parents or siblings could be more difficult. The long term effects of the divorce are still not completely gone and probably never will be, but what I have taken away from this experience, I consider a tremendous asset, which has helped me grow as a person to who I am today. I could not imagine going through the trauma that I went through as a child growing up in a divorced family. I felt as though I was an outcast because all of my friends' families were still all together. I was unable to experience the father–son relationship that most of my friends had grown accustomed to. I felt as though I was not good enough in sports and not confident enough to realize that I did have talents. Not being confident caused me to be the person who was picked on because I always made mistakes that would not have been made if I would have believed in myself, as I do now.

As I grow older I have found acceptance and happiness through what has happened through my parents' divorce. While I have found happiness, I still find myself questioning all the relationships I have been in. I want to make sure that I do not make the same mistake my parents made. I could not imagine going through another divorce (my own), or seeing future children of mine having to go through the situations that I was put in at an early age in life. Divorce is something that should be experienced by no one. For the people who are going through this right now all I can tell them is to believe, believe that the divorce is for the better. It does not matter how difficult it may seem, eventually all of the pieces will fit together and they will realize how great life really can be.

CONCLUSIONS

Listening to the voices in this chapter, there clearly is hope for the children of divorce. Many have adapted, and well. Many have gained maturity beyond their years. All have grieved. Many have used their grief in positive ways in developing their own perspective about their parents, the contingencies of living, and in beginning their own careers of close romantic relationships. Many have learned that parents who are just hanging onto relationships for the family's sake was not a compelling rationale for living, and the family was better off when the formal union was ended—leading to new arrangements that turned out to be less strife ridden and more constructive for the adults and children involved. Many have found their own evidence for Ahrons's (1994) argument that, indeed, there can be "good divorces" that leave the humans involved intact and growing. Finally, the narratives in this chapter reinforce the notion that there can be positive adjustment changes over time and that, for many people, time is a healing factor.

It seems obvious from the narratives in this chapter that young people want the loving support of both parents, but they also want straight answers about the possibility of divorce when it seems imminent. As children age, they deserve to know (at least some of) what is happening in marriages that affects them. One respondent in this chapter noted that she knew her parents' marriage was in trouble, but she needed to know what the parents were thinking about the possibility of separation and divorce. Parents' honesty in dealing with children may help the children adjust and develop more positive views of the decision-making process. The narratives also suggest that when children are provided some information on why the divorce occurred they seem to have an easier time in later "forgiving" their parents for perceived transgressions and in developing a mutually satisfying parent–child relationship. This final quote, from a 22-year-old man, best summarizes the hopeful message that a good percentage of young people offered about their parents' divorce:

There's no doubt in my mind that divorce has had a major impact on my life. The ironic thing is that if I could change what happened or some of the things that I went through, I don't think that I would. Everything that I've been through has made me stronger and more self-reliant. It's improved my relationships with my siblings and made me into the person I am today, which I'm happy with. I wouldn't wish the experience of divorce on anyone, but I feel that in a way, it has made me a better person.

CHAPTER

5

BECOMING "FATHERLESS" BECAUSE OF DIVORCE

*My father lived fifteen minutes away from me and would not come
visit ... I haven't talked to my father in over 3 months and it
hurts every day ... I really want a relationship with my father, but
I think the divorce has made him disown me.*

—22-year-old woman

*Children and young adults keep the absent father in mind forever.
Often when they reach adulthood they go in search of him. The
child who feels abandoned by her father suffers a great deal.*

—Judith Wallerstein, radio interview, December 19, 2000

These quotes speak to the special feelings of loss associated
with a child's feeling of abandonment by a father, or any parent. A
litany of loss language surrounds many divorces. On many occa-

sions, the greatest sense of loss is caused by the absence of a father in the life of the child. There are books and movies with titles such as "Daddy Doesn't Live Here Anymore," "Where Is Daddy?," and "Will Dad Ever Move Back Home?" In a smaller number of stories, the mother is absent, but usually she is the caretaker who is still available. Children mourn the loss of their parents, and there now is a substantial children's literature on the loss of parents. Because most of the parental losses reported in this book (as well as by children of divorce in the general population) involve fathers, we focus in this chapter on the loss of a father because of divorce.

The major themes identified in this chapter are presented in Table 5.1, which shows that the themes focus around the loss of one's father, including less frequent contact and less meaningful involvement. However, the themes also illustrate that the consequences of losing one's father are compounded when the student perceives that he or she has had to assume additional responsibilities in the father's absence and/or if the student experiences the death of a sibling. In the stories that follow, young people tell about their experiences in feeling virtually "fatherless" as a consequence of divorce.

"TOO LATE"

A common theme in students' stories of lost fathers is that the fathers disappear near the time of divorce and at some extended later point want to renew their relationship with their children. However, it is often too late. Lost mothers sometimes are themes

TABLE 5.1
Major Themes of Father Absence From Students' Narratives

- Fathers' attempts to become more involved are "too late"
- Father became too busy
- Losing a father early and then sporadic involvement
- A "double loss" of father
- Death of a sibling, then loss of a father
- "You're the man of the house now"
- Hope mixed with loss

too, but not as often. Many fathers may absent themselves from their children's lives because of their feelings that they have been wronged by custody agreements or by alimony (i.e., spousal maintenance) awarded to the mother. Sometimes, these disappearing fathers may be substance abusers, or they may be chasing after new romantic/sexual partners. Any number of other factors, not well identified in these narratives, may influence how active the father, or a parent in general, is in the lives of children.

The first story in this chapter is emblematic of the pattern of the lost father who is too late to come back into the child's life. In this account, a 22-year-old woman describes her feelings that in time have become deep anguish, as she has tried and failed to make contact with her father, who seemingly could never love her after his divorce from her mother. She reflects both a degree of alienation often expressed by young women whose fathers have gone away after a divorce and an orientation to her own close relationships that involves "taking no prisoners" in her expectations of men she dates. Perhaps most important, her narrative illustrates the theme that it may be too late for previously absent fathers to enter their children's lives in a meaningful way. Although only one story reflecting this theme is presented, it was a common element of students' narratives. This one reflects well the various stories exemplifying the theme of the father "being too late."

When my parents told me they were getting a divorce I was only 4 years old, much too young and naive to know the implications it would have on the years ahead. I responded to their words by asking for permission to play at the neighbor's house, while my 7-year-old brother could not even utter through his tears. My mother eventually decided to arrange for my brother to attend therapy, although I suspect he has still not fully recovered and hides his pain with his hardened personality.

My mother initiated the divorce proceedings when her tolerance of my father's alcoholism ceased. She wanted the best for her children and my father was never there to help her raise and nurture us. He had desired another son when I was born and could never find a way to bond with his new daughter. My mother noticed his actions and made an extra effort when she was with me. It must have hurt her to see me try so hard, even still in college, to create a relationship with my father where one could never exist.

When we moved to Iowa 2 weeks before my freshman year in high school I said good-bye to my father, although I had no idea it would be one of my last face-to-face conversations with him. He arrived at the house, late as usual, that day to sign papers granting my mother full custody of my brother and me. He signed, without hesitation. We took a few pictures on the front lawn and then he was gone. Without a tear in his eye, it was almost as if he had already severed the relationship he had with us long before that day.

My sophomore year in college I attempted to correspond with my father. I justified one last effort by telling myself that I wouldn't forgive myself if I hadn't tried and then found out one day that it was too late. I sat down at my computer in my dorm room and began to write him an e-mail. I asked him all the difficult questions to which I always wanted answers. Did he wish to even be a small part of my life? Why did he never initiate contact? The list went on.

A few days after I wrote, I received a response. Indeed he wished to be a part of my life, he said he wanted to be a large part. He claimed he had no excuse for what had happened in the past, just that he was sorry. While years before this date I would have been thrilled with his statement, it was now much too late for him to want to get so involved. He had already missed so much of my life and the effort seemed to great to fill him in for what I would receive in return. He had missed my school plays, father–daughter functions, birthdays, graduation, holidays, the list goes on at length. Certainly he had excuses for not attending those events through the years. Usually it was that he had to take an exam to get his Master's Degree. I must have heard that excuse a dozen times, but to this day still haven't figured out how he could get his Master's without having an undergraduate degree. He had plenty of excuses then, but he was never as sorry as he seemed in that e-mail.

We communicated via e-mail for a few months, exchanging a few messages. He told me all about his life, but never asked about mine. I was hurt, but later that summer I decided to give him a chance to redeem himself in a conversation over the phone. I kept his number for quite some time before calling. I was not sure what I would say. How would his voice sound? Would he recognize me? Would he be too busy to talk? Putting all these questions aside, I finally picked up the phone, I hesitatingly dialed and hung up. I was nervous. I tried again. I picked up the phone and slowly dialed, but hoped he would not be home. The operator came on the line, "this number has been disconnected and is no longer in service" she said. He had escaped contact with me again.

I have not talked to my father since I tried calling him that day, nor has he continued e-mailing me. I do not know what his voice sounds like. I do not know if he is truly sorry. I do not know where he lives or even if a memory of me remains through the years of alcoholic lies and apologies.

While he may not be physically visible, he has certainly had a great influence on my life in regards to relationships. I no longer trust people as easily and innocently as I once did. I have learned to value proof when excuses are given. Most of all I have learned to value integrity in a man above all else. I do not date men simply because they are attractive as many college women do. I have high expectations for every man I date and if at any time in a relationship I cannot see myself ever marrying that person, I break [off] that relationship because the effort seems wasted. I am not quick to commit and I know that the man I marry will be one whom I date many years before engagement.

I am sure I have hurt a few men along the way, but refuse to live the life of my parents. I could never live with myself if I knew that someday a child of mine was listening to the arguments from around the corner. Too many have already lived that horror.

Comment

The foregoing narrative has several interesting secondary themes embedded within. Common to many of the narratives in this chapter was the young woman's yearning and searching for her father; she had some success with e-mails, but then he neglected her again—even e-mailing proved to be too much for him. Still, there seems to a yearning in this woman for her father. As is often the case, searching behavior accompanied this yearning. She has become a savvy analyst of his excuses for why he could not be there when she had special events, and she has become somewhat of a cynic in the process. She also indicates that she has learned to be quick to decide whether men are right for her. As she says, she probably has hurt men by leaving them quickly and abruptly—dating qualities that she attributes to her "missing dad."

FATHER BECAME TOO BUSY

The following account, written by a 20-year-old woman, illustrates another common theme: The father becomes too busy to have a relationship with his child. This narrative also further highlights the "too late" theme.

Eventually he "became too busy," according to my father, to take our visits any longer. He still sent us birthday and Christmas cards with money enclosed and stopped by every once in awhile. Then everything stopped for a few years. Neither my brother nor I had any contact with him, and he never saw us. The next time that I did see him I was probably 15 or 16 years old and was with my friends at the supermarket. I ran into him in the parking lot and all he could say was things to belittle me. He asked if I was pregnant, if I was still working fast food, or if I had flunked out of school by now. He made me feel about one inch tall and embarrassed me so much in front of my friends. He wasn't even happy to see me. Luckily, my friends stuck up for me and told him to "fuck off" and took me away from him.

The next time I saw him was at Wal-Mart my junior year in college, where I endured the same treatment. This time, though, I had a lot more to say for myself and told him exactly what had gone on in my life concerning college, and my career just to prove to him that I was going somewhere in life. Both times I've run into him at the store, he was buying beer. So much for AA.

My brother sees him every once in awhile because he stops by his house, but my father never calls him. My brother and I have different perspectives on him. I hate him for what he has become and how he treats me now, but my brother hasn't given up on him. My father didn't come to either one of our high school graduations, and that was the only time I ever saw my brother cry. I'm debating whether to send a notice of my own graduation in December, not because I expect him to come, but to once again prove what he's missing out on.

Hopefully sometime down the road, I hope he realizes what he has missed without having his children in his life. He never remarried and still lives 10 miles from my mother. He has no other children, no excuse.

My mom remarried a man years ago and is now happily married. My stepfather never replaced my own father, but he was the only father figure I had to look up to. I am grateful that I at least had him.

Comment

The preceding account again shows a disdain that develops for the father who is uninvolved in his child's life. This reaction makes sense in light of this woman's encounters with her father, whom she felt assumed the worst of her. Not so subtly, she hints at his drinking problem. Note the young woman's point, however, that her brother has not given up on the relationship. She apparently has. She just wants him to know that she has had successes, despite what he apparently has assumed about her.

LOSING A FATHER EARLY, THEN SPORADIC INVOLVEMENT

The following woman, age 22, reported a type of sporadic relationship to no relationship with her father that began early in her life and that, unfortunately, too many young women have experienced in their first 20 years. It should be noted again that missing special "father–daughter moments" is a painful recollection for this woman, as it is for many others.

Divorce has affected me since I can remember. My parents separated before I was even born and then got divorced when I was 2. My father had a drug problem and put my mother, my sister, and myself in danger with his habit. After the divorce my father was not in the picture. I have never asked him or my mother but I assume he was still using drugs and wanted nothing to do with us, at that time. Around fifth grade he suddenly came back into our lives. He was living in Florida and had stopped doing drugs. During the time he was "gone" my mother raised my sister and me on her own. My sister is 4 years older than I am and she helped to raise me because my mom worked 2 jobs. My grandma, my dad's mom, also helped out, a lot. I'm sure it was out of a sense of responsibility, because my father was not around. I remained very close to my father's side of the family when I was younger. My sister and I spent holidays and many weekends with my grandma.

Seeing as how my father was never around when I was young, I never had a chance to develop a relationship with him. I never got a chance to have all those father–daughter moments. He was never there to coach my little league team or teach me how to throw the ball like a boy. It was very disruptive for him to suddenly come back into my life. He just expected me to accept him. It was easier for my sister because she had memories of him and knew him as a father. I on the other hand was just supposed to start being his daughter. I am a very strong-willed person and didn't accept this instant relationship. I did try to get to know him but he is a very hard man to know and love. To this day we don't get along that well. He still lives in Florida and is in a serious relationship, with a great woman. She does a lot for him and for my sister and me. My father comes home a couple of times a year, mainly for Christmas and my grandma's birthday. We do talk once or twice a week on the phone but they are very superficial conversations about the weather and the football team.

The only good thing that came out of my parents' divorce is my extremely close relationship with my mother and sister. I have the utmost respect for my mother and all that she sacrificed for us when we were younger. The 3 of us stick together and watch out for each other. My mom has since remarried a wonderful man, who I consider my dad. He has been around since my 7th-grade year. He loves my mom and treats her like she has always deserved to be treated. He loves my sister and me like his own children. He is the one I call to tell about a great grade on a paper or a new guy. He has changed our lives.

The fact that my father wasn't around when I was younger has affected my relationships with other men, though. I have a fear of being abandoned by anyone I get really close to and I have a tendency to push people away. I am starting to see that not all people leave ones they love. I see it constantly with my mother and stepfather. I am very lucky to get along so well with my stepfather. I still miss the relationship I could have had with my father but I wouldn't change the one I have with my stepfather.

Comment

The foregoing account reinforces the abandonment theme that other women suggested had come out of their feeling of missing their fathers. Furthermore, this woman clearly reiterates a very common pattern: her relationship (or lack thereof) with her father has had strong negative effects on her current relationships with men. This narrative also shows how many children of divorce have a feeling of great respect for and protectiveness of their mothers, whom they do not blame for their fathers' neglect. It is also noteworthy how complimentary she is of her stepmother, appreciating how good she is to the same man towards whom she feels some ambivalence.

A "DOUBLE LOSS" OF FATHER

The following account changes the tenor somewhat of this set of themes of a neglectful father. In the following story, written by a

22-year-old woman, the father apparently is prevented by the mother and stepfather from playing much of a role in the woman's life; then death occurs, doubling the sense of loss for the young woman. This narrative shows not only a young person's great loss and pain in the turmoil of divorce but also her great courage in dealing with both divorce and death. After her parents' divorce, and then a period of estrangement and separation from her father, her father suddenly died. Thus, her grief was doubled, and she feels greatly cheated by life's course of events.

My parents divorced when I was going on 4 and my brother was 7. At this early age I did not understand what that meant. I cannot really remember any of the details of that time. I barely remember my dad.

My mom got custody of me and my brother without a fight. We were told, among other things, that he [our father] did not want us ... My dad moved across the state. Those first few years I knew nothing of him, where he was, or what he did. At that age I was oblivious to the reality of being without a dad. My mom knew too well the realities. My dad was supposed to pay child support, but rarely did, and never the full amount. My mom was strapped trying to raise two kids on her own.

In what I would describe as desperation, my mom moved us 2 hours away from the rest of our family to a bigger town so that she could find a better job to support us. She did this with a male friend that she and my dad had known for a few years. We all lived together, rather poorly. After a few years they decided to get married. My brother and I, now 8 and 12, respectively, were strongly against him. We felt she did not need him, we did not like him, and he was definitely not a substitute for a father figure. This was very confusing to us because we thought our dad did not want us. This was reinforced from the bad mouthing that went on around the house about my dad. My mom was bitter towards our dad, but most of the bad mouthing came from our stepfather.

It seemed like my brother and I were being turned against our dad. We were poor and supposedly this was my father's fault for not paying proper child support. Later I learned that he could not financially help that. We were allowed to visit with him, when he showed interest. This was very awkward. I was young and rarely saw him. He was like a stranger. A stranger I wanted to love because he gave me life. But I was scared and resentful.

My substitute of a father was not a good one. I hated him for not trying to control my brother and me, and for verbal abuse. He even ran my brother out of the house at age 14, so again I was abandoned. I felt cheated when my friends had good dads, where there were father–daughter activities, and when holidays came around. We would sometimes get Christmas gifts, rarely on birthdays. I did not get to know my dad's side of the family at all. I would write my dad letters and send him school pictures. I would get a few responses back filled with love and excuses for everything. He was remarried and had a new life and I felt excluded from them. Though still too scared to go stay with him, he was starting to come around in a long distance manner.

The last time I saw my father he was dropping my brother back off at my aunt's from a visit. It was awkward, short; we couldn't even visit. But he hugged me for a long time, cried, and told me how much he loved me. I was scared and confused. It was not more than a few years after that he died of a heart attack at age 45. I felt guilty for not knowing him more. I did not get to grieve properly because my parents didn't really like him and people thought I should feel so sad because we weren't close. He was still my dad! My brother was just starting to come around to him. I blame myself, but I was so young, so I also blame my parents for brainwashing me. But I can't forget to blame my dad for not being more active in our lives.

I don't even understand why they got a divorce. My mom probably will never fully explain it, and that's OK. But I always wonder what life would have been like if I had a real dad, a real home, and a real childhood. I feel cheated, angry, and resentful. I hope that my relationships aren't affected. I strive to be healthier and happier than I ever was growing up. I vow to make things better in my own future marriage and for my future children. It is nice that divorce isn't such a secret now. I had no one to talk to. All of my friends came from good homes and my brother wasn't there. I think my childhood was cheated and that I went through a lot that I have taught myself to forget. It is easier for me not to think about it. Sometimes I forget that I went through it all, that it wasn't normal, that I missed out. At times the void feels normal, to not have a dad, it is part of my reality that few understand. I lost him twice. I don't know what it would have been like to have a real dad. How would things have been different if none of it had ever happened?

Comment

This account is quite unusual in that death also contributes to the feeling of abandonment. Note, too, that the woman sounds the familiar theme of concern about whether her close relationships will be adversely affected by the chain of circumstances, including a poor relationship with her stepfather. Furthermore, she indicates concern about her lack of knowledge of why the divorce occurred and her mother's reluctance to explain the reasons for the dissolution to her.

The next account in this section also describes the pain felt by a young woman, age 21, who lost her father first to divorce and then almost lost him to death in an accident. This account shows how young people usually do not want to lose their fathers on a permanent basis. This woman says that she cannot hate her father and hopes for a reconciliation before she has children, so that they will know their grandfather.

When I was 13 my parents decided to get a divorce. I would have to say that I had a pretty good childhood, although my father was never around. The reason that my parents divorced was because my dad was having an affair. It all started in an on-line chat room. Most people would just blow it off saying that it is just a phase that he is going through because of mid-life crisis. It was on my dad's birthday that he decided to leave us with our vacation money. I didn't know what to do. My mother was crying constantly as well as my younger brother. I didn't really do much. I didn't tell any of my friends what was going on in my life even though that I should have. It probably would have made me feel better if I would have. After that year my relationships with my friends started to change for the worse. I isolated everyone from me, including the person who needed me worse, my mother.

My dad moved to Kansas City on that day and he stayed there just over a year. For the first several months I do not remember my father calling me or else I never talked to him by choice. For a long time I despised my dad. I never (and still don't) understood why he left. I thought that everything was going good in our lives. I talked to my dad off and on and saw him maybe once a month for the next five years. This really didn't bother me and then he did something that made me so angry that I did not talk to him for 3 months. I became engaged when I was 18. I know that I was young and had my whole life in front of me but I just felt that it was the right thing to do. I didn't tell my dad for several months because I knew what his reaction would be. Somehow in the little town that I'm from my great aunt found out and told my dad what she had heard. So it was time for me to 'fess up and I did through an e-mail. He wrote me back telling me how disappointed he was in me and that my boyfriend should have been a real man and asked my dad for permission. I was so mad because for years my dad was never there and I felt that he had no right to tell me what decisions needed to be made.

Then a few months later my dad was in a terrible accident that nearly killed him. Unfortunately, it takes the loss or almost losing of someone to really realize how special they are to you. I then took care of my dad over the summer and formed a better relationship with my father. Now that it has been almost 2 years since my dad got into the accident and 7 years since my parents' divorce, I still resent my dad for doing the things that he did. I never thought the things that I do now. I don't understand why he did the things that he did and I probably never will. I can't hate my dad forever so I guess that I just have to let some things go and move on with my life because one day I will have children of my own and I don't want them to live their life without knowing their grandfather. I just wish that he would stop thinking about himself and put his children first for once.

Comment

This account shows the possibility that even missing fathers can be found—albeit, in this case, in the unfortunate circumstance of a serious accident. This account reinforces the idea that young adults may need to persevere to achieve relationships with fathers. It may be worth the effort, and sometimes disappointment, to do so. In this case, it is noteworthy that this young woman's motivation for her continued efforts to maintain a relationship with her father at least partially seems to stem from her desire to provide her future children with the kind of family stability (i.e., her children having a relationship with their grandfather) that she found lacking in her own life.

DEATH OF A SIBLING, THEN LOSS OF A FATHER

In this final account, which deals with death as a part of the experiential package, a father is depicted as never recovering from the loss of a child and then other deaths. The author, a 21-year-old woman, tells how her father apparently took out his hurt and anger over a series of deaths on the ones he loved. This set of events led to divorce and, in effect, the children's loss of their father. This story is one of a highly disturbed father and how his violent behavior (that also involved sexual abuse), reflecting considerable psychological problems, left a huge burden of pain on his family after he left.

I have been directly affected by divorce in my life. When I was born in 1980 my life was pretty normal. My family lived in Iowa and my father worked and my mother was a stay at home mom. My mother was loving but my father was always a little cold towards his children. Early on my father had lost his father to suicide and his mother to cancer. After both of his parents died, he isolated himself from the rest of his family. When he met my mother he appeared to be normal, but he was a little bit controlling.

Things drastically changed in my family when my younger sister was born in 1983 and then passed away later that day. After my sister's death, my father was never the same. He was isolated himself from everyone and he began to beat my mother. He also began to become very strict and controlling. I can recall every day before my father came home from work; we had to spend an hour cleaning and organizing the house to make sure it was perfect for him. If it was not, my father would beat my mother and sometimes my sister up. Small things would set him off, like a toy on the floor or a can in the wrong spot in the cupboard.

In 1987 my father became increasingly violent after his best friend died of a heart attack. The cumulative effects of the losses were more than my father could handle, but he still insisted on internalizing everything. Two days before Easter and a month after the death of his friend, my father snapped. He began to yell because the canned food had been put away in the wrong spot. I sat underneath the oak dining room table and watched in horror like I had many times before. My father took everything out of the cupboards and threw it on the floor and then grabbed a loaf of bread and smacked my mother across the head with it. My older sister came running up the stairs and my father punched her square in the face. I continued to hide underneath the table with my brother Tom, paralyzed with fear. I heard my mother cry out in pain as my father repeatedly hit her in the face. My older sister tried to pull my father off of my mother but her attempts failed when he pushed her to the ground. My brother and I sneaked to the phone to call the police and we told them to come quickly. We crawled back under the table to wait for help. Finally after what seemed like hours they arrived. My father answered the door and pretended like nothing was wrong; then my mother smiled and nodded to agree with him. The police left, satisfied with their attempt to find out what was really going on. My father went to his room for awhile, but after an hour came back for seconds. He started beating my mother again but this time he laid into her with no remorse. He finally picked her up and tossed her headfirst into the door like a sack of potatoes. She didn't move and neither did I because I was so shocked at what I had just witnessed. My fa-

ther did not even check to make sure she was all right; he just walked out the door and slammed it shut. I remember running to my mother's bloody, limp body and thinking that she was dead. Finally she came to and we went to the ER and then we checked ourselves into a hotel for Easter.

Soon after this event, my mother filed for divorce. This was not a shock to me; in fact I was happy that my parents were getting divorced. I feared that if my parents had stayed married my mother would die eventually. What I did not anticipate was how messy a divorce could actually be. I became a tool to my parents; they used me as leverage to get things they wanted and to harm each other.

On occasion my father would stop by the house; when this occurred I would often feel betrayed because my mother would be so nice to him. It became very confusing for me and I was not sure how to act around him. Soon after my parents' divorce, my father began to sexually abuse me on unsupervised visits; one day my brother walked in while this was occurring and he told my mother. After this another court battle took place. My mother's lawyer promised me that I would not have to testify. On the day of court I was notified that I would have to testify. I cried and pleaded and eventually got my way, however my mother was not happy. She pulled me aside and told me that if anything ever happened to my brothers or sisters it would be my fault. This statement essentially ended my relationship with my mother. So now I do not have relationships with her or with my father. I have spent years trying to cope with my losses that occurred in my youth and it has been a difficult road to recovery.

Comment

The foregoing account is one of many in this book describing the difficult journey of a young person in a family filled with discord and instability. This 21-year-old woman and her siblings endured sheer hell growing up, yet she is open and brave in making her statement. She feels estranged from both parents. Her father has reportedly carried out deeds that are so despicable that she may never be able to forgive him. And she no longer is close to her mother because of further events that transpired in the course of violence, abuse, and court-related hostility. Indeed, by merely telling this story as part of our project, she is exhibiting tremendous courage. She is doing well in college and hopes to graduate soon. What will be the future of her relationships with her parents? Unfortunately, because of a lack of research evidence on this issue, only time can answer this question.

"YOU'RE THE MAN OF THE HOUSE NOW"

In the following account, a young man, age 22, tells the story of his father leaving the home and putting him in charge as the "man of the house." He describes the arduous passage to the present and how that passage has made him a strong, independent person. This man had to grow up essentially without a father to guide him.

Looking back on my childhood I cannot recall a time in which my parents were happy together. What I do recall though are explosive arguments between my father and mother that usually had to be broken up by my older brother, while I locked myself in my room trying to block out the reality of what was happening outside my door. Being young (in elementary school) I believed everything would subside and my parents would find a way to make their marriage work, not realizing that both of my parents were suffocating in the relationship and desperately seeking ways in which to end the 18-year marriage.

I was 10 years old when my father came to me and informed me that my parents were getting a divorce and that he would be moving out of our house for good. I was very upset because of course I thought this meant he was leaving town forever to never be seen or heard from again. But he soon reassured me that he would only be moving several miles away (in order to keep his job) and that this final separation would be better for the whole family. Initially he was right. The house was more calm and I no longer had to come home to a war zone. I began to feel relieved that my parents were divorced because they were both happier and both were excited to get on with their new single lives. But the more my parents began to reinvent themselves as single people in the community, the more I began to realize one of my fathers' final warnings before he left, "Brent, you are the man of the house now. Housework, lawn work, and taking care of your mother, you are going to have be responsible and learn how to take care of yourself."

I was now in sixth grade, my brother was beginning his first year another university some 3 hours away, and both my parents began to date and continue to work full time. This left me at home the majority of the time by myself, cooking meals, cleaning and maintaining the house. The duties that my father took care of were now put onto my shoulders and at the time I felt that I was losing out on the fun of being a regular junior high student. All of this time caring for the house and home needs resulted in me distancing myself from my peers, who I felt did not suffer the hardships that I did. On the weekends while my friends were skiing or playing football I had to remain home and help my mother and do odd jobs around the house. Throughout junior high I felt that I had lost the opportunity to be young and free. I did not see these new responsibilities as life lessons, but as repercussions from my parents' divorce.

Now at age 22, I realize how beneficial those years of quick maturity and early independence have been in the development of my character. I have found meaning in my parents' divorce, that is, it allowed me to become an independent and responsible young man early in my life. It taught me that loved ones will be there for you, but you must look out for yourself and not always rely on others to accommodate your needs. I have a stronger sense of independence and have learned how to take care of myself and my responsibilities. A lot of people my age could not honestly say that they could take care of themselves. So even though I lost a parent through divorce I gained a character and a strong personality that will be with me forever.

Comment

By happenstance, the preceding account is the only one in this chapter written by a man regarding a young person incurring new adult responsibilities in the home. The fact that this account was the only one in this chapter written by a male student may reflect either: (a) some continuing gender differences in how males and females are expected to take charge of certain household duties, with the male carrying a heavy burden of domestic duties, and/or (b) that females are more used to fulfilling certain household tasks and thus find it less disruptive when a greater household burden is placed on them after divorce. Although this man indicated that he missed out on having meaningful contact with his father after the divorce, he was glad that he had carried out these duties. He clearly perceives that he lost out on some of the fun that his peers were having, but now, years later, his conclusion is that this experience of having so much responsibility has made him a better person and at the same time resolved a conflicted marriage that was a huge burden for him and his brother.

HOPE MIXED WITH LOSS

In this longer account, a 21-year-old woman describes the loss of a father and how much she has gained from her relationship with her stepfather, a theme we noted in chapter 4. Her story is filled with links to the relevant literature on divorce and its consequences. Such a strong set of links to the literature was found frequently in these accounts. It was as if the writers were seeing their own lives in the ideas and findings of scholars in the divorce field. They were highly motivated to understand that literature and to see if it had relevance to their experiences.

Examining children of divorce and its outcomes is a very intriguing topic for many, especially since the divorce rate is so high. There has been great disagreement about divorce and the impact it may have on children. Ahrons, in "The Good Divorce," states that divorce can be civil and cooperating with each other as colleagues can protect the kids. Others describe how divorce puts responsibility on children, such as taking care of younger siblings. According to Judith Wallerstein, it may be better to stay married if it is good enough to stay in order to avoid adverse effects of divorce on children. As a child of divorce, my life makes sense of some of these theories and makes others seem irrational. Most importantly, theories aside, looking at my life as a child of divorce can teach others and myself many lessons about life.

In order to grasp the extent to which the divorce has affected my family and me, it is best to start at the beginning of the end. My parents dated from middle school on, and were always considered the "perfect couple" by their peers. Immediately after high school, my parents married. Very shortly following, they went from being a young married couple to young parents. They divorced when I was only 2 years old, after a 2-year marriage. As I am told from relatives, my parents had a very rough time. Today my mom still says, "We were young and gave up too easy probably." My father was abusing alcohol and became verbally abusive towards my mother. She would tell me stories of hiding in the closet from him when he went on a drunken rampage. She decided that she did not want to live like this and left him.

Consequently to my mother's decision, I was part of a broken family very young. Probably because I was so young, I have very few memories of my parents when they were together or of the divorce. However, I do remember the house that my parents lived in very clearly. My father designed the house himself and had it built when my mom got pregnant. I can close my eyes and walk through the house and even describe to others details such as the color of the carpet. Another memory I have is of sitting in a beanbag with my father watching morning cartoons together. It is the single image I have of him and I together when my parents were married. The only other memory I have is my mother and me leaving the house with my father waving goodbye to me from the top of the stairs as my mother cried. Many do not believe me when I describe this because I was only 2, but I know my description is accurate. Some say that these are not memories at all, but images I created over the years. I know in my heart that these memories are real.

Despite my age, I was grieving when my parents divorced. According to Harvey, young children may show disenfranchised grief most clearly. People do not acknowledge what young children understand or feel during these times of loss. As Harvey describes, they may not have the experience to know how to grieve. My mom said that at the time she told me, "Mommy and Daddy will always be friends but we are not going to live together anymore. We will always be there for you." This was probably the best description she could have given me of divorce at age 2. However, I missed my dad and was sad that my mom was crying so much. So much attention was given to her that I was shielded from the "bad stuff." This idea of disenfranchised grief also relates to the memories described above. People don't believe that I remember the events at the time of the divorce, just like they think that I was too young to understand the divorce enough to feel loss.

Maybe as a result of the disenfranchised grief, from the divorce till about age 10 or so, I thought very highly of my father. During those years, no one ever said anything bad about my dad. My mom would listen with a smile when I got excited after my father called. My stepfather never interfered with my constant letter writing to my dad despite the fact that I never got a letter back. My mother would take me shopping for my dad's birthday, knowing that I would never receive a birthday card from him. I feel that I lived in my own fantasy world for those years. I think that my mom and stepfather were trying to protect me, but I wish that they hadn't. I was in a state of denial about the role of my dad in my life. He was my dad and that was all that mattered to me for so long. I was filled with so much curiosity about him, and created a super-dad image in the place of the reality.

The reality about my father is that he did not fulfill any fatherly duty. He joined the military immediately following the divorce, and I have seen him only 4 times in the past 20 years. His absence causes me great pain and re-

sentiment to this day. I can't pinpoint the moment I began to reverse my feel-ings for my dad, but he was no longer the super-dad I made him out to be. I was assuming that a father would love his daughter, be a part of her life, and to be there for her when she needed it. These assumptions were shattered when I began to open my self up to see what my father was really like. These shattered assumptions hurt everyday of my life.

The visits I have had with my dad have changed over the years. There is not much that has changed about the way he acts, but I judge him differ-ently now than I did when I was younger. One visit I had was still in my "super-dad" phase. He was in town for a few hours and took me shopping. We went to the toy store and he let me pick anything out I wanted. At the time I thought my dad was the best. I was so excited about the toy, and said, "Thanks Daddy" as if I saw him every day. On the contrary, my most recent visit with him consisted of dinner with him and his family and did not have such a loving and forgiving theme. The whole situation was awkward be-cause he is a complete stranger to me. He knows very little about my life and nothing about my personality. When he tried to offer to buy my dinner or even refill my soda, I refused. I just kept remembering how [the] toy he bought me years ago was used as a shield to reality. I did not want him to buy or bribe my love, or even my attention.

The best way to describe the past 8 years or so is an emotional roller coaster. Before my current revengeful state, I really wanted to get to know my father. I decided that if he was not going to be the one to initiate a rela-tionship then I better start interacting with him or it would never happen. I tried to e-mail him a few times about what I was doing with my life, such as where I was working and whom I was dating. I really just wanted to learn more about him and to let him see what kind of person I was growing up to be. When my father first remarried, I had a very hard time getting any attention from my father. His new wife was Korean, and held strong family values. She did not believe in divorce and had a difficult time even deciding to marry my father because he had a previous wife. She did not want my father and I to have any contact because I was a connection to his previous marriage. I am not sure to this day if my dad was using this as an excuse to continue his lack of involvement in my life or if his new wife re-ally felt this way.

By the time I was 16, my father made a brief turnaround. He was living in Texas at the time and sent me a ticket to come see him for a week. I could not believe it. I was so happy and yet so scared. I had not seen him since I was 9 years old. I was afraid of his expectations of me since the last time he saw me was as a young child; not a teenager. I was afraid about what we would talk about and how we would get along. Despite my hesitations, I went to see him. As soon as I got off the plane in Texas and saw him waiting for me I began to cry hysterically. It was such an amazing feeling to hug my father. There was a connection between us that cannot be broken by time. I just wish that we would utilize that connection.

While visiting him, my father and I had a great time. He took me site-seeing for most of the visit. We were always out doing something together. We were both afraid to have to just sit in a room together and talk. I was enjoying my time with him so much that I did not want to discuss our relationship and history. On the other hand, I also wanted to scream and swear for a few straight hours and let him know how I had been hurt over the years. I made it through the week without displaying any bitterness or anger. My father and I both have very energetic and humorous personalities, which worked well together over that week. I just wanted to stare at him as much as I could because he was my dad. The feeling I had while staring at this stranger and knowing that he was my father is almost indescribable. I wanted us to be [a] "normal" father and daughter, but I knew that it would not ever be that way.

In addition to visiting with my father at this time, I was getting to know my half-brother and half-sister. The girl was 9 and the boy was 5, and this was the first time I had ever met them. I was an only child at the time in my mother and stepfather's household, so they fascinated me. I love children and always wanted younger siblings, so the fact that I kind of had two was different. The girl called me her big sister, and was bragging to all of the neighborhood kids. I had so much fun playing with her, even though it was very awkward for me. Just like my father, these siblings of mine were complete strangers. However, the fact that we had the same father was enough for us to get along all week and act like family. I care a lot for Sarah and Alex and wish that I could see them more often. I wish that we had had the opportunity to grow up together rather than apart. I understand that the distance in miles between us would hinder this to some extent, but my father's reluctance to include me in his life is more to blame.

Overall, this visit was entertaining. I had a good time with my father and siblings, but it unfortunately was more of a show than reality. We did get to catch up on each other's life to some extent, but it was impossible to get to know a person in a week's time. I was hoping that this visit would initiate more contact between us, but that proved to be otherwise. Once I left Texas, life went on as before. I had to realize that my father wanted to play the fun guy role with me at his convenience, which turned out to be every 5 years or so, and play the invisible father act all the years in between. I had been getting an occasional e-mail from him every few months that just said hi. I would reply with long letters telling him all about life at the time. I became very frustrated at trying to let him in my life and getting little response from him. I sent a final e-mail to him asking him to write e-mails to me that tell me about what is going on with his life rather than small talk. For example, I found out from my Grandmother that he had broken his leg. I told him over e-mail that I would much rather hear about these details than getting the generic, "Hi. How are you? I am fine," e-mails. My request failed miserably and I do not hear from him via e-mail or otherwise anymore.

I think that I have reached a point where I want justice. I despise the fact that I was so forgiving for so many years. He never sent a birthday card, never congratulated me when I graduated high school, or participated in any other life events with me. Similar to family member who lost a loved one through violence and want the perpetrator punished, I want my father to suffer as I have for all the pain he has caused. For example, when my grandmother, his mom, asked him when he was going to get me a plane ticket to come see him, he said, "I have to spend my money on my kids now." According to him, I am not his child anymore now that he has 2 new ones. I wanted to scream when I heard this. I am and always will be, whether either of us likes it, his daughter.

I have a very extensive history of letdown with my father. I have tried to make the best of it over the years, but I have given up. I am very tired of his broken promises, especially his most recent promise to have me come visit him again. He told me that my high school graduation gift would be a ticket to Hawaii, where he is currently living. I am now a senior in college and he is still talking about getting me this ticket. I know that it will never happen. I am low on his priority list in life. As a result, I have put him lower on my priority list. I am not e-mailing him anymore. I am not sending birthday or Christmas gifts or even cards anymore. Just once I would like a card or phone call from him saying "Happy Birthday," especially since he is one reason I exist today.

My ploy for justice has a deeper twist to it than the obvious neglect I am going to give my father. I discovered about 4 years ago that I have another half-brother. Apparently, according to my grandfather, my father had a fling with a woman between his marriage with my mother and his current wife. The result of this fling was a baby boy. This baby boy is now in his teens and has no idea I exist. He had contacted my grandparents, our father's parents, because he wanted to know his father. This son attempted to write my father, but my father threw the letter out. He then called my grandparents and denied that the boy was his and told them to tell him not to contact him. Unfortunately for my father, the son is the exact image of my father. The resemblance cannot be ignored. I feel for the son because I get the same rejection from our father even though he acknowledges me as his daughter.

As I was indicating, I would really like to show my dad the pain he has caused. I have been debating for the past 4 years to find the son and take a surprise trip to Hawaii. My father's wife does not have any knowledge about the other son. He is getting child support taken directly out of his military paycheck, but she knows nothing about it. Given her strict Korean beliefs about marriage and children, knowledge of the son would surely end their marriage. There is a part of me that would really like to spring this on my father so he can have a taste of what it feels like to be left and ignored. However, I cannot bring myself to such a horrible act. As a consequence, I have made no effort in contacting the son. He still does not know that I exist. He is my half-brother though. I go back and forth on what would be best for him and when I consider contacting him. I still don't know what to do. My inability to decide is a decision in itself because I have not contacted him yet. Maybe someday I will meet him.

Despite all of these complications, my father's family and I have always been close and continue to be close. This is one of the most unique aspects of my parents' divorce, and many people are in awe of how well it works. When my parents first divorced, my mother vowed to keep my father's side of the family a part of my life no matter what choices my father made. Today my mother describes this to be one of the hardest parts of the divorce, "It was hard to lose that family. At least we do have a great relationship, other than sharing our everyday lives together." Even after my mother remarried, I was also taken over to my grandparents on the holidays. This has continued into my adult years. Every holiday I drive from my mother's parents to my father's parents to my stepfather's parents. My holidays are very hectic, but I love having so many supportive relatives.

My stepfather helped create a home for me with two loving parents. Even though my biological father was an insignificant part of my life, my stepfather fulfilled every fatherly duty in his place. My mother tells me her thoughts on children and divorce: "It affects a child through divorce no matter what age. I think that you are a stronger person today because I am married to Greg. Greg and I gave you self-esteem by encouraging you at everything you do or did. We were there for you when you got an A on a test and when there were rough times." I agree with my mother. The many low points of the relationship between my biological father and me and the disappoint-

ments I have endured have made me stronger rather than weaker. The support and the love I felt from those around me kept me from becoming the child of divorce that Wallerstein describes.

In addition to my strong character, the divorce has instilled in me other traits. Most of my pain from the divorce is directed to my father because he chose not to be a part of my life when I was a child or as an adult. For this reason, I feel very strongly against young marriages. My parents had been dating since middle school, but were not ready for marriage at age 18. I think that they each needed to live a part of their adult lives independently before marrying. Knowing that they could stand on their own would have allowed greater love and security together. This may explain why I strive to be my own person and not to depend on others to the point that I would be not be able to live without them.

The best lessons in life about a relationship have come out of my parents' divorce. Being a part of a "broken home" allows me to see what a relationship needs to last. This may help me avoid unhealthy and hasty relationships in my own life. I am engaged to be married to a man I trust and love deeply. I carry no fears of ending up like my parents because I was able to learn from their mistakes without living through them myself. My mother says, "Greg and I have a loving relationship that you will see in your own relationship. You grew up in a good home in which there was respect and love." I am confident that my marriage will be very healthy for both my husband and myself. In addition, I know that our children will be loved and given the attention that they deserve.

Overall, being a child of divorce has given me much pain, but also many gains. I will continue to struggle with my father for years, but I have the support of his family, my stepfather, and all my other friends and family in his place. I am grateful for the lessons I have learned about respect, relationships, and unconditional love. I will instill these values in my life and my future.

Comment

This account reflects considerable growth and at the same time ambivalence. The ambivalence is manifest, on the one hand, by the woman's allusion to feelings of revenge toward her father for his inaction when she reached out to him and for the acute feelings of hurt that his perceived abandonment caused her. On the other hand, she also to some extent protects her father and his current nuclear family by not telling her stepmother about her half-brother, which she suggests would certainly end their marriage. She has chosen to protect her father and his family despite the fact that, as she suggests, she has lots of reasons to be angry about her father's neglect. She writes eloquently about the enduring bond that she feels toward her father, despite his distancing behavior. Nevertheless, her grief is palpable and filled with piquant and painful memories. She literally is expressing a catharsis of emotions at points during her account.

Overall, as she said, children grieve their parents' divorce for years, well into their adult years. She was hurting and angry, even as good events were surrounding her current life. Nevertheless, she was tired of reaching out to her father and his current wife and their children and feeling little reciprocation from her father.

This woman ends her account with a positive assessment by emphasizing how her mother, stepfather, grandparents, and other family members have helped her develop strength in her relationships (with an impending marriage) and to feel good about herself. It does seem clear from her account that much of her strength in early adulthood stems from these loving interactions with different family members. It seems clear, too, that her mother and some key family members are open to talking about the effects of divorce on her life and their lives in general. She stresses her appreciation of the role of this openness and regular confiding behavior between her and close others in helping her achieve the maturity that she now feels and the confidence to soon enter into a marriage of her own that she trusts will be "healthy."

CONCLUSIONS

Before discussing major conclusions, we should emphasize that fathers' behavior and inaction often were criticized roundly in the narratives in this chapter. However, we did not hear from these fathers. There are always multiple perspectives on every situation, particularly in emotionally laden family events that have taken place over many years. Thus, it is quite possible, if not likely, that the fathers would tell stories that present themselves in a more favorable light. They probably would often speak of being unfairly treated in custody decisions.

Nevertheless, as we have stressed throughout this book, and in our defense of the narrative method, it is the students' genuine and forthright recollections and accounts that most strongly influence their reactions to their parents' divorce. Thus, although it is possible that some accounts reflect one-sided or exaggerated negative views of the fathers' behaviors, the vividness and clarity of the accounts suggest to us that they are likely to be largely veridical with external reality to the extent that we can know it at this time. Some fathers' behavior likely reflected their sense of guilt in abandoning their children. Others may still have not cared enough about their children and the fathering role to do the job that their children felt was their duty. Whatever the case, we do not have the fathers' accounts to study. Thus, the motivation behind fathers' behavior is a critical and missing link in our understanding of the "fatherlessness" experience as revealed in this book.

Leaving aside the fathers' perspectives, two interrelated conclusions from the children's stories are plausible: (a) fathers are needed in the lives of children and (b) perhaps more important, children feel a great sense of loss when their fathers are not involved in their lives after divorce. Many fathers are mourned because of their absence in their children's lives. However, even though they may experience a sense of loss and mourning for their father, many children of divorce seem to do fine in continuously single parent families, with little or no fatherly influence. Furthermore, stepfathers often do a good job of filling in and even being the major father figure in the child's whole life to this point.

Nevertheless, we would hope that biological fathers would listen closely to these stories of pain. Many of our respondents strongly assert that loving father figures have been vital to their well-being and success in early adulthood. Highly engaged fathers apparently help children live more stable and constructive lives and do better in school and community activities. Conservative author David Blankenhorn (1995) concluded in *Fatherless America* that fatherlessness is a primary generator of violence in America among young men. Although there are almost certainly a multitude of causes of violence among young men in addition to a lack of father involvement, the stories here clearly attest to these young people's continued faith in the role of the father in preparing them for life.

They also attest to the abiding grief associated with fathers who are "missing in action."

"My parents got divorced when I was 4. I didn't understand it then. I only knew my dad was never around ... My dad didn't love me (my mom made excuses for him). He didn't even want to have me. I have such resentment towards him ... How could he be so removed from me and the family for so long?"

—Woman, age 21

CHAPTER

6

FAMILY CHAOS AND RESILIENCE

I am a child of divorce. Having said that, I don't consider myself defined by this category by any means. I have a very supportive family and I have never felt as if I was missing something.
—Man whose story is told in this chapter

This chapter focuses on families and their complex dynamics in the context of divorce. It contains stories that reflect well the mixture of perceived chaos and resilience in the minds of so many young people who have experienced divorce in their families. It shows that, even in painful divorce circumstances, there is a complex mix of feelings and outcomes. These positive and negative experiences may occur simultaneously. This amalgam of experiences is shown to a greater degree in the stories in this chapter than was true in the narratives of earlier chapters. The chapter narratives also included diverse commentary on the role of family in the divorces being described. In this chapter, however, the centrality of the family comes into even sharper focus in the stories.

Table 6.1 presents the major themes found in this chapter. As shown in the table, these themes all have an underlying dimension of struggling to cope with very complex and complicated family situations.

STRENGTH IN APPRECIATION OF COMPLEXITY

The first, lengthy story shows the uncommon maturity that many young people have had to learn as they deal with the instability in the lives of their elders. The author, a man, analyzes in a sophisticated way the ups and downs associated with his own intricate family dynamics. He models a strength others in similar situations can readily appreciate when he spins his story more toward the "glass is half- full" metaphor than the "glass is half-empty" metaphor. As readers will see in the details of the narrative, it seems quite understandable that he feels overwhelmed by way too much instability and desertion among the parental figures in his life.

This story, written by a 21-year-old business student, also focuses on many of the issues faced by adult children who have experienced multiple parental divorces. It also highlights a theme that we have seen several times in earlier chapters: Nonbiological parental figures may play a more important role in the adult child's social support system than do biological parents. In addition, it also shows how siblings may have quite different experiences and reactions to divorce-related events.

TABLE 6.1
Major Themes of Family Chaos and Resilience

- Finding strength and willpower in highly complicated family situations
- Surviving multiple divorces
- Pretending that the family is "normal"
- Struggling to cope and the imperative to mature, and quickly
- Difficulty accepting a stepfather
- Finding sanity in a chaotic world

In September of 1977, I was born in a small town in the Midwest. I had one sibling, a sister who was 8 years older than me. My father was employed as an assistant manager in a local grocery store and my mother was employed in a factory. I believe that my life was pretty normal until one day in August of 1985. That day my mother said that she was "going on vacation," and moved into an apartment across town. Four months after this, my father and mother were officially divorced and she moved to a large nearby city.·In 1988, my father would marry a woman from my town, named Pam. In 1995, he would leave Pam and me and move in with another woman. "At present, approximately 50% to 60% of all kids under the age of eighteen will spend some part of their childhood in a single-parent household." So, before I reached the age of 18, I had endured two divorces. In this paper, I am going to discuss how I adapted from this sense of loss of family; and I will compare it to how my older sister handled the same event.

In January of 1986, my parents were divorced. My mother moved to the state capital, leaving my father to take care of my 16-year-old sister, Jessica, and me. To gain the facts in this situation, I tried to interview both of my parents. I was unable to reach my mother, but I was able to speak to my father about this divorce. He said that my mother told him "that she was 40 years old, and have never been on her own in her entire life, she always had someone telling her what to do." Shortly after the divorce, my father began to build a social support network; he did this by attending a divorce-support group that was started by the local junior college. Shortly after joining this support group, he began dating my future stepmother, Pam.

At my young age, I did not cope with the breakup of my parents very well. In the interview with my father, he stated that I blamed myself for the divorce. This reaction to divorce is backed up by research done by Wallerstein and Kelly. They state that the child believes that something that they had done had caused a fight between the parents and that this one fight led to the divorce. My social support network was not very strong either. My father worked a full-time job and had to put in extreme hours, sometimes not getting home until after midnight. My relationship was not good with my sister, who because of the divorce was asked to do extra things that she did not have to do before. From kindergarten through 6th grade, I attended a Catholic school. I was in 2nd grade when my parents divorced, and out of my class of 15 I was the only one with parents who had divorced. This disrupted my social network tremendously, because I was teased and harassed by some of my classmates. The teasing was not all due to my parents' divorce, but also was due to my behavior after the divorce. Shortly after the divorce, I began to twirl my hair, which caused some of it fall out, giving me a bald spot on the top of my head. I remember crying myself to sleep many times during the immediate period after the divorce. It became so bad that my father sent me to talk to the priest of our local parish. Some time went by, and my life began to stabilize. With the introduction of Pam into my life, I began to recover.

My sister Jessica handled the divorce differently from myself. The biggest adjustment that she had to make was due to the rise in the amount of responsibilities that she had to assume. Responsibilities such as cooking dinner and cleaning the house, chores that used to be shared between my mother and my father were now shared between her and my father. During the interview with my father, I asked him to describe the relationship between my sister and my mother after the divorce. My father said, "It was not very good. Jessica told me not to take her back, if she wanted to come back, 'because she would just leave again'." As for Jessica's social support network, it was still very strong; her friends were very supportive. However, when I interviewed my sister for this project, she believed that the divorce was an improvement. She and our mother did not get along, and she mentioned during the interview she only remembers one motherly moment from our mother. However in the interview with my sister, I asked her how this divorce affected her social relationships and although she was not unhappy when our parents were divorced, she did admit to some lingering issues. She said that if she is having trouble in a relationship or if she is bored, she does not try and work it out; she just lets it go.

During this time, my mother had visitation rights with me, but my sister never visited her and rarely spoke to her. My relationship with my mother held on a lot longer. For the first couple of years after the divorce, I visited my mother once or twice a month. But, as time marched on, I visited less and less frequently until she moved to a southern state in 1995. There were many reasons for the decline in visits as time passed. For one thing, the visits became less and less enjoyable. My mother had very little stability in her life. She was bouncing around from low paying job to low paying job, and she rarely kept the same roommate for more than a few months. Her social life was very unstable as she went from relationship to relationship. As her son, I had to meet many of her partners, which was a very uncomfortable experience as many of them were not someone you would like to see your mother around. I can recall two occasions where a situation with one of her friends or partners resulted in calling the police. As I became older, I started limiting my visits due to other weekend social obligations.

After the divorce, my father, my sister and I started spending more time to-gether and as a family unit, we began to get closer. While the relationship be-tween my mother and her children deteriorated, the relationship between my father and his children was growing. According to research, the daughter is more like to suffer from separation anxiety and research also stated that many children long for parental reconciliation. I know that in the begin-ning, I wanted my parents to reconcile; but my sister never did. I think that I wanted reconciliation all the way up until around the time of my father and Pam's engagement.

As my father and Pam began to get closer, other situations started to de-velop. My sister did not immediately accept Pam into the family and there was some hostility from Jessica's side. I am not exactly sure why there was hostility, because Jessica was supposedly not unhappy about my parents' di-vorce. I was not very pleased with the thought of having my mother replaced. Generally, I had the same reaction when my mother introduced to me one of her various boyfriends. However, as it turned out, Pam was a very calming influence in my life. She was 11 years older than my father, and already had three grown-up sons and seven grandchildren. As time went by, Pam and I became closer. Our relationship withstood many problems, such as one of my mother's friends spreading a rumor that Pam and my father had been hav-ing an affair.

In 1988, my father and Pam were married. By this time, Jessica was in the middle of her first year at a nearby college, and I was in fourth grade. My father and I moved into Pam's house out in the country. My father and Pam seemed deeply in love; something that neither my sister nor myself could re-member from the first marriage. From the beginning, Pam tried to instill some discipline into me, by giving me weekly chores. Although sometimes we did not see eye to eye, she became more my mother than my real mother. In spite of this, I have never called Pam "Mom."

Even with all of this, this marriage had its share of hardships. In 1989, my grandfather on my father's side passed away due to a stroke. This af-fected my father strongly and he began to visit his mother who lived 40 miles away even more than he had previously. In 1992, his mother was diagnosed with colon cancer and it was at that time, the doctors determined that it would be fatal. Over that summer, my family and I visited the hospital at least five times per week. In an interview with Pam, she stated that during this time, "we had stopped having fun." My grandmother died in 1992. Unfortunately, before the marriage could heal from my father's terrible loss, it was dealt another hardship. Pam's oldest grandson, Bob, had been hav-ing trouble at home, especially with his father. About a year after the death of my grandmother, Pam's grandson moved into our house. There was disagreement between Pam and my father over the situation. Pam wanted to help out her grandson and my father wanted Bob to go back and try to work it out with his father. My father was never a healthy man; he was diabetic, and had high blood pressure. For his ailments, he always had to take medication. This, coupled with his irritation over the Bob situation, started placing some strain on the marriage. Of course, I did not realize the severity of the situation.

One winter night 1994, I came home from a night of hanging out with my friends. My father was playing Solitaire on the computer and we chatted for a little bit. As I was about to go off to bed, he told me about this woman that he had met, whom he enjoyed talking to about his problems. I remember looking at him strangely and said to him, "Don't mess this up. We have a good thing going here." That is the last I heard about his other woman for a little while. Until one Sunday in 1995, I came home from playing football with my friends and he told me that he was going to move out. This sort of surprised me, because I had no idea that there was any problem; other than the one night that he mentioned the other woman. Bob had moved out in the summer of 1994. I talked to him for quite awhile about not leaving Pam, and told him to just work things out. I thought that I had him convinced. A few days later, in 1995, he met me as I was leaving work and told me that he was moving out and moving in with this other woman.

On that 15-minute drive out to Pam's house, I thought about what had started in 1985 had finally ended in 1995, the destruction of my family. My sister was at her college, preparing for law school, my mother was in the South, and my father was "shacking up" in some woman's house. I did not have a family; I worried about what might happen when I returned to Pam's house; whether she would want me around or not. As, I walked into the house, there was Pam crying and she gave me a hug; and that is when I knew that my family had not been completely destroyed. She was going to allow me to continue to live with her. Over the next few days, I saw what my father's leaving had done to Pam.

My irritation turned to anger, which eventually turned into rage. No longer did I accept my father as my dad, and I began to call him by his name, Joe. For the rest of my stay in my hometown before I came to college, I had very little contact with Joe. With less and less contact, I became more and more angry with the man. The anger culminated one night in 1995, when some friends and I egged his house. As I look back on it, it seemed like a very immature and futile gesture, but at that point it seemed more ceremonious than anything else. At that moment, I had washed my hands of him.

My sister Jessica took this divorce a lot harder than the first divorce. In the interview with Pam, she said that Jessica took the divorce very hard. Jessica had said that she did not have a family anymore and that she felt like an orphan. Before the divorce, Jessica and my father were very close, but it destroyed their close relationship, although she did answer with the same sort of anger that I did. This is very important in the fact that she was on her own and was not even involved in the immediate situation as things went down.

After the divorce, Jessica and I became closer to the parent that did not leave. Jessica, Pam, and I became very close, much closer than we had been previously. During this time, the relationship between Joe and his children had become almost nonexistent. Before the divorce, Jessica used to speak to him at least once per week; now she only speaks to him once every couple of months. Even then their conversations are not very serious, generally they are about sports or another unimportant topic. After I left and went to college, when I did come back to hometown, she was the only parent that I visited. I never went and visited my father. It was very rare that I even spoke to him, only when he tried to call me and I was not doing a good job of screening my calls. It would not be until 1999 that I forgave my father. I have not really forgiven; it is more like that I just understand what he did. For the past 2 years, our relationship has been getting stronger, but it will never regain the strength that it had before the second divorce.

In October of 1997, Joe would eventually marry the other woman, Gene. I did not go to the wedding; I received an invitation and shortly after, threw it in the trash. I have never met my new stepmother, and I have no intention of ever doing so. Although, I do now understand what Joe did, because she was much younger, I still have quite a bit of rage towards her. Even now, I do not visit Joe, because I do not want to have a chance meeting with this woman. For the most part, other than phone conversations, the only contact that I have with my father is that my sister and I will have dinner or lunch with him on the day after Christmas. Never Christmas Day, because that day is too important for me.

I do not really have a relationship with my birth mother either. Between the ages of 15 and 17, we did not speak more than once a month. Although when I gave her news of Pam's and Joe's divorce, she came up to our hometown. That is when she told me that she hoped for [a] reconciliation with Joe. Obviously, the reconciliation never materialized, which was a good thing. Jessica and I talked about how far things had come, because if that reconciliation had happened, neither of us would want to be with them anyway. At this time, my relationship with my mother is very distant. I do not want to be with her at all anymore. Our relationship is still very tele-phone-dependent. Jessica's relationship with my mother is far worse; she has not spoken to my mother since 1999. Jessica does not want her to have any part of her life.

I have discussed in this paper how divorce has shaped the lives of two people. My sister and I have dealt with two divorces, at the occurrence of each divorce we were in different stages of our lives. I was 8 years old when my parents were divorced and I was devastated. The divorce shook my self-esteem and put my life into a spiral. It was not pulled out of the spiral, until my father started seriously dating Pam. I was 17 years old when the second divorce occurred. This divorce did not damage my self-esteem; it made me worry more about the future of my family. I reacted with a lot of anger towards whomever I felt was the guilty party, which was my father. It would take me over 4 years, before I could understand what he had done.

Jessica was 16 when the first divorce took place. She reacted then much the same way, I did during the second divorce. She too was very angry with who she felt was the guilty party which was my mother. She has yet to try and understand what my mother did, let alone forgive it. She has not spoken to my mother since 1999. She was 24 years old when the second divorce occurred. She took this divorce much harder and thought herself an "orphan" because of what my father had done. Although, I cannot back it up with any scientific research, it does seem that teenagers lash out with more anger during a divorce that people of different age groups.

I am uncertain of the total effect that these divorces have had on my life. Certainly, they have not scared me away from marriage. One day, when the time is right, I do plan to marry. I am not afraid that I will be "[like] father, like son" with my future wife and end up leaving her and my future children. If there is anything that these divorces have taught me it is that there is more to family than being related. I do not feel any sort of relationship towards either of my parents, other than maybe friendship. I will not depend on them ever again, for anything. My former stepmother Pam and her family is my family now.

The effect of the first divorce on Jessica was that it caused her not to fight for her relationships and if that it just became too hard, then she would quit. I feel that I am exactly opposite in regards to relationships. I will fight to make a relationship work, and I will try and work through the problems that my partner and I might be having. Rather than just calling it quits. The second divorce also affected Jessica's views on relationships negatively. In the interview that I conducted with her, she told me that due to her father cheating that she really could not trust men.

Also, it made her think that everyone has his or her own agenda, so you can only rely on yourself.

Now with the holiday season fast approaching, I am planning on doing things with Pam and my new family. With not even a thought towards either of my birth parents, although I will probably send my mother a card and maybe buy my father a present. So, that we can exchange them on the day after Christmas. Upon occasion, I wonder what my life would have been like if the first divorce had not taken place. As, I look back on it, I am glad that it took place. I am very pleased to have Pam in my life and I know that she has had a major hand in shaping what I have become today and for this I will always be grateful.

Comment

This discerning story was told by a young man in his early 20s. He shows the maturity of a person much older. He probably has had to develop such maturity to survive and even thrive, as he has done in school. His family literally already has had the "many exits and many entrances" of which Shakespeare wrote. Many more may yet occur in this respondent's life. Through all this instability, he has maintained his composure in analyzing who really is his family. It is remarkable that he has selected his ex-stepmother and her new family as his "real family." He sees this family on holidays and not the current families either of his biological father or mother.

There are other interesting aspects to this narrative. Note that the respondent interviewed different family members. This step was common in this project. It shows the extent to which the respondents cared about knowing how their different family members had felt in the painful moments of family despair surrounding divorce. Note, too, that this young man is quite concerned about and protective of his sister, who apparently has not survived with as much optimism as he shows.

Most important, the young man poignantly points to the anguish in many hearts and minds about the frequent family changes that he and his loved ones have experienced.

The following, briefer stories also show how pain connected with divorce in the family often is transformed in time to penetrating insights in the young person's outlook on life and close relationships. The "glass is half-full" metaphor about how to look at the unfolding of divorce situations can be found in these stories, too.

MULTIPLE DIVORCES

As was evident in the preceding account, multiple divorces have their own dynamics of pain and instability. With second and later marriages ending in divorce almost 60% of the time, this experience is becoming all too common for many children. The following account reflects a 21-year-old woman's experience of multiple divorces by her parents.

I am a child of divorce and here is my story.

There was a long time in my life where I couldn't ride in a car after dark without feeling as if I would never go home again. I felt I would never see my family again and as if life would never be the same. I would be forced to remember that I would never know the carefree life again, that I used to live. Every time I got into a car these thoughts would ring through my mind. When I was 8 years old my parents separated. They had filed for a divorce and we were moving away from the only home and the only family I had ever known. We packed all our belongings into a semi-trailer driven by my uncle and the five of us, my uncle, my mom, my 2 sisters and me, began what proved to be the longest journey of my life thus far. We drove from the South to Iowa where my mom's family lived. I had visited them but they were still strangers to me. Mom had made us each little packages to keep us busy. I remember the dry-erase board and markers that were to occupy my time. And for a period of my life the smell of those markers also reminded me of that sadness. We didn't drive a lot at night in the first year after my parents were divorced. We lived in town and Mom worked in town. It wasn't until we moved 2 years later that I realized how much of an effect that divorce still had on me. The odd sick feeling I had in my stomach when we drove after dark. I was still feeling it. I knew my life had changed. I went from a carefree 8 year-old to a mother in 2 years [in taking care of her siblings]. My mom went to school part time and had work–study jobs and internships. In 2 years I learned how to cook, clean, do my own laundry and raise my kids/sisters. That is what they were to me, my kids. At age 10, I had already learned more about being a parent than anyone with a baby knew. I learned about family hardships, financial instability, welfare and broken homes. I knew more than any kid my age should have had to know. And I was my mother's confidant. She told me how she felt, what she was going through, and all the troubles we were facing and were going to have to face as a family. I started hating my dad. Not from anything she had directly blamed on him but because I thought he had it so easy and I felt he had put this burden on me. I didn't have to baby-sit in my former home. Life was simpler there, or so it seemed to me at the time.

    After another year life got better. My mom got her degree and I realized I never wanted to go through college with kids, I had already done it once. We moved to a new town, one of the many moves I had experienced within the last few years of my life. I had started unpacking only half of my belongings. If I only used it sometimes, I could find it in a box. I didn't want to have to pack again in 3 months. I was getting used to the idea of having only one parent, or so it seemed. And this is the most profound moment I remember experiencing that made me feel as if I had truly lost something and someone in my life. This is when I knew that other families were different. Now it still seems like a trivial thing but the meaning behind it and all it represented at the time meant so much to me. I was going to Girl Scout camp over part of my Christmas break; still on welfare, we had scraped and saved for me to take this trip. I remember lying in my bunk crying my eyes out with my face pressed into the pillow because I was the only girl without a stocking; why, because you were supposed to bring one of your dad's socks. I felt so alone and empty. And to cry over something so trivial as a sock, I felt like such a child. Too bad no one was there to remind me that I was just a child. I had done so much growing up so fast; I forgot what it was like to be a child. Camp ended and my counselors used a coffee cup instead of a sock. I lived through it.

    Life went on the same as before, I did laundry, dishes, cooked and cleaned and mom worked insane hours to make ends meet. It was the least I could do to help around the house and to watch my sisters. Needless to say between my limited cooking skills at the age of 12, and the limited groceries we had and that were supplied to us, I am now probably one of the pickiest eaters anyone has seen. We lived off what was cheap and/or provided, and ramen noodles, Hamburger Helper, and pot pies now make me gag. Peanut butter, macaroni, chili, beef stew, any thing that was given to us by welfare and that we had to eat repetitively, I won't touch still to this day.

    It wasn't until about 2 years after camp that I experienced what most children of broken homes experience, remarriage. My mother got remarried. My father had gotten remarried the year before and I didn't approve of the woman he married, her being the one for whom he left my mother for. But it didn't have a large effect on me since I only saw him 2 months out of the year. With my mom it was a different story. The biggest thing for me [was] the name change. Everyone assumed my mother's name was the same as mine. I hated it when someone called me Minnie or called my mom Mrs. Smith. I hated that they just assumed those things; it was odd how much that meant to me. Now I just laugh it off when someone calls my mother or me by the wrong name and I have found it useful in identifying telemarketers. Well now I love my stepfather dearly. He is the kindest, funniest man and I am so glad my mother found him. Although I sometimes feel like I am on an episode of the Brady Bunch. He has four kids from a previous family, and my mom has three, so we have one too many. And of course being Black, it doesn't help that my sisters all have blonde hair.

Last November I experienced a second divorce. Like I said my father's remarriage didn't have a huge effect on me but his divorce leveled me for a few weeks. Every time I thought of what had happened I just had so much anger. His wife, my stepmom, left him. Just up and walked out saying she wasn't happy. I was worried about my sister. She had been living in the South for about 3 years, and my stepmom was slowly becoming a mother figure to her. And my stepbrother, what was to become of him? My father was the only father he had ever known. But most of all I was angry because I trusted her. It took me so long to learn how to love and to trust again after what had happened to my parents. I didn't see the point in emotional investment because I thought it all led to hurt. And I had trusted her, it took me 8 years but I had moved beyond the point of tolerance to almost love for her. I trusted her and her leaving me ripped my heart out. I didn't understand. There I was back at square one, feeling as if I was 8 years old and lost again. I got over the anger but it still hurts. I think of my stepbrother abandoned by his mom and wonder how he must feel. He dropped out of college, lost his job and took up smoking. And I wondered what was going to happen to my sister; her grades had dropped and she was in another one of her depressive states.

So my family survived its second divorce. And I think I tolerated it better when I was younger. Which bring me to another point I would like to address before I close this piece, the issue of staying in a relationship for the sake of the kids or divorcing. My mother's parents didn't separate until she was 40 and it had a huge effect on her. She didn't know how to share her time between them and felt she was being unfair when she drove to visit and only saw one of them. Kids don't think like that. I never thought I was being unfair to my father when I only saw him 2 months a year. And my best friend from my hometown—her parents are separated and in the process of getting a divorce. She feels as if her whole high school career was spent just living in a lie. So my position on this debate [about whether unhappily married parents should stay together for the sake of the children] *is that I would stand with those who believe you should divorce, because an unstable unhappy home life isn't going to help the situation any. I just think they need to implement better programs for those who have to go though divorce, be it in financial assistance or emotional.*

Comment

This narrative is another amazingly insightful story about a family saga that has occurred in the decade or so since this woman's parents were divorced when she was 8. The complexity of events, not unlike those of the first narrative in the chapter, is staggering to comprehend. Yet, she too is surviving and finishing her college education. Note the potency of economic deprivation in her family and how she had to play the role of a motherlike figure in interactions with her siblings and to be a confidant to her mother.

One may wonder what the long-term effects of this saga on this young woman will be in the next few decades. Will she be an exceptionally strong woman who can handle whatever life throws at her? She seems very strong now. Or will she be feeling the fall-out from so much responsibility as a young person? Given the lack of available research evidence on such long-term effects, it seems too early to predict her later course.

PRETENDING THAT THE FAMILY IS NORMAL

In the following story, a 20-year-old female nursing student discusses a common theme in problematic family life, namely, pretense. Families sometimes have a very difficult time admitting to their many warts— much less trying to make the best of them. Conflict and struggle bring out the folly of pretense very often in these families.

I have spent the majority of my teen and adult life pretending that my life was normal. I am growing up in a time when half of all marriages end in divorce. Why shouldn't my parents' marriage end the same way? With so many children of divorce as my peers it seemed silly [not] to share my experiences with others who had gone through the same type of dissolution. Why should my situation be an exception to the rule? I convinced myself that my life was relatively normal and dealt with it as if what had happened in my life was not a life-altering event. This is partially true, and also quite false.

None of us could face the truth and talk about it. We lived a life of pretense in presenting a public persona that all was fine in our family.

The divorce of my parents was not the most difficult of situations I faced growing up, and not life-altering by itself. I knew that my parents had been fighting and I knew that financially we were continually digging a larger hole that we weren't sure we could climb out of. The actual announcement of my parents' divorce was not a large shock. I remember crying, but I also remember not really knowing why. And I remember moving on in my new apartment with my mother and my sister and without my father. That was comfortable and okay.

The dissolution of my relationship with my father began long before my parents decided to divorce; so one thing is not contingent upon the other. I have only recently begun to realize that I am tied to a family experiencing the reproduction of loss. My life is a prime example of the effect that loss can have on one person, and how it can persist to affect others. My father and my mother both have experienced significant loss that continues to haunt all of us to this day. My father's losses specifically relate to the loss or absence of my relationship with him. However my father's disengagement began long before the divorce of my parents when I was 13. I am a fatherless child, and that is why my situation is different.

Through the processes of account-making and discussion I have started to understand the impact that this perpetuation of loss has had on my life. Even more so, I am beginning to understand how the experiences that both of my parents endured have affected them.

This writing project has provided me the opportunity to continue telling my story and in turn work on healing the pain I have experienced. My personal journal has been a journey for me to understand myself and I see this project the same way. Not only can I safely discuss topics too taboo for verbal discussion, but also I am provided the opportunity to continue my account-making process, which has proved therapeutic for me thus far.

Comment

The foregoing narrative overlaps with narratives in chapter 5 in that this woman feels "fatherless." It shows not only how unraveling families sometimes try to pretend that everything is fine and normal in their family but also how some young people have come to see divorce as almost a "normal process" in society. It is too frequent, and it happens often in the lives of friends, especially if one has an extensive friendship network. However, that does not make the divorcing process or its consequences any less hurtful. Note, finally, that this woman's relatively brief account suggests that she is only now beginning the "account-making" process, whereas the first two respondents appeared to be experienced in this type of analysis. They appear to have been account-makers about their family lives well before they heard the term in one of the classes in which respondents entered this project.

THE LONG STRUGGLE

In the following story, a 21-year-old male psychology student describes the common theme of having to struggle for a long time to cope with divorce in his family. This struggle is filled with practical as well as psychological/emotional dilemmas. Similar to the respondents whose stories were chronicled in chapter 4, he shows the derivative positive spirit that characterizes many children of divorce who have found the strength to survive these bewildering events. Note also that this story shows his considerable gain in maturity as the process unfolded, even though his father has apparently chosen to be absent in the long run. Thus, again, we have a mixed-type story with yet another respondent feeling the loss of a father as well as the losses of a type of family life he had anticipated having in the future.

I am a child of divorce. Having said that, I don't consider myself defined by this category by any means. I have a very supportive family and I have never felt as if I was missing something.

I was born in Iowa and my father was there for at most a few months. He then moved to New England to start a new job and the rest of my family was to move out later after he got settled. When I was 1 year old we all moved to New England. My mother said that I was never comfortable going to him after that. We lived in two towns in New England and then when I was 4, my mom found out that my father had started an affair while he was there alone and it went on for 3 years before she found out and wanted a divorce. My mom, sister, two brothers, and I then moved back to Iowa. We stayed with relatives until my mom found a house in a large city in Iowa and could start working full time (about *a month). The woman my father had been having an affair with had 3 children; he has adopted her children. Since then, I have seen my father on 3 separate occasions over the course of 18 years. For much of the time my parents have been divorced, my father didn't pay any child support. The point at which his negligence had reached approximately $30,000, my mother took him to court. During that time, he declared bankruptcy and therefore was not responsible to pay. When he regained employment, the court ordered his wages garnished. Since that time my mother has received the same minimal amount each month and he has offered no other assistance.*

My mother is a very religious person and that has been a large part of her survival, but it also contributed to some of her pain. She felt a lot of guilt about her marriage failing and still struggles with the issue of forgiveness. She was able to get an annulment and has made progress towards forgiveness, but she still has much resentment. She says that my father is an indecent man. I am positive that my mother was a happy woman at one point in her life, because I see glimpses of it often. However, it is hard for her to hide the marks of a tired, overworked, wounded woman. The ironic thing is that all of her continued resentment is related to the years of non-involvement romantically and lack of responsibility that my father has shown towards my siblings and I—not for the awful treatment he showed her. Any resentment I have is not because I don't have a father, but because the way this man treated my mother makes me sick. I have struggled for a long time trying to figure out if it is worth my time and effort to foster a relationship with my father, because what I have now is not a relationship in the least. The contact I have had with my father has been in the form of a call on my birthday and Christmas along with a card ... and now it's usually just a card. I've always felt that my conversations with my father were similar to a conversation I would have with a friend of the family who was calling for someone else, but in so doing he would find out what I was up to. After each call, I would always wonder why I didn't yell at him and tell him all the reasons that he has been a terrible person.

There is no denying that the divorce of my parents had a very large impact on all of our lives and continues to do so. However, the impact is not entirely negative. As far as I'm concerned, I never had a father and therefore don't miss having a father. The relationships that I have with my mother and my siblings are incredibly fulfilling and positive and I can't imagine having grown up any other way.

Comment

This narrative is a thoughtful statement about the loss of a dad in a young man's life and about the losses wreaked on his family life by his father's departure to be with the woman with whom he was having an affair. One has to wonder if the final comment about not missing his father is true. He almost sounds as if he is protesting too much and that he greatly misses his father being in his life more substantially—at least as a father acting more responsibly toward his siblings, mother and himself. Moreover, his empathy for his mother is quite apparent. He describes her as "tired, overworked, and wounded," hurt as much by her own lack of a romantic involvement as by the loss of her husband and his neglectful ways in (not) supporting his children. This empathy toward mothers was fairly common in the narratives, especially among respondents who felt the loss of their fathers.

THE IMPERATIVE TO MATURE

In the next narrative, a 22-year-old pre-med student addresses the imperative that many children of divorce encounter: They have to mature to meet life's challenges, and their maturing cannot take too long.

I am a "child of divorce." It's like saying I am an alcoholic, it's very hard. My parents separated when I was a freshman in high school. It wasn't until I was a senior that the divorce papers were filed and signed. Sometimes I feel like they are just still separated, so it's hard to admit I am a child of divorce. It's even harder when I am walking down the street or sitting in a restaurant and I see the traditional family. The mother and father happily married, and the children being able to share quality family time as a whole, instead of having separate occasions to be with both parents. It's uncomfortable at times, and the jealousy can be overwhelming.

In Give Sorrow Words, *Dr. Harvey talks about a sense of loss of family origin or a "normal life condition." This loss overwhelms me at times, and led me to believe that what is supposed to be a normal life condition is not. We are supposed to be a normal family like everybody else, but we are not, and neither is everybody else. It takes a long time to realize that there is no such thing as a normal family, even if you believe that your family is so far from the norm, that normal can be any family that is not like yours. I don't have a normal life, and what I used to think was normal, never really was. The breakup of my parents started long before the separation, and has lasted well after the signing of the papers.*

My parents separated twice. The first time my father moved out; this was when the feelings of abandonment began for me; this is when my relationship with my father deteriorated. When he left he didn't tell me he was leaving, he didn't call me, tell me where he was living, or give me a phone number until almost 6 months after he moved out. I felt at this time extremely abandoned, I felt unwanted, like my own father didn't want me to be in his life anymore. Why couldn't he call me? I think what made this even harder for me was that he told my brother and sister where he was and he called them, but he never called me. It's like he was scared because I was old enough to know what was going on and he just decided by not talking to me that he was doing my a favor.

My dad moved back in a year later, and even having him back at home we didn't talk. I was very upset and angry with him, I figured if he couldn't have kept in contact with me when he left, then I didn't need to keep in contact with him either. I thought, "Well he's the dad, he should make every effort to be with his kids," and when that didn't happen I didn't want to be with him anymore. About 6 months after my dad moved back in, my mom moved out. My sister and I moved in with her, and my brother stayed with my dad. My brother had moved in with my dad when he left the first time.

It took my mom the next 2 years to finally file for divorce. The divorce process was more trying on us kids during that 1 year than the whole 16 or 17 years we had witnessed our parents fighting. The divorce was ugly. Money was a big issue, possessions was even a bigger issue. Even though my mom gave my dad the house we had lived in without a fight, my dad still thought he was getting cheated in every way, and that's not my assumption. The few times I would see my father the only thing he would talk about is how my mom was screwing him over, and then in return my mom would talk about how my dad needs to grow up and take on responsibility. It was endless mud-slinging. The name calling, the he said, she said, the countless accusations. They were both guilty of this, and they still are even 3 years later. I guess I've just come to ignore most of what they say about each other to me.

While the divorce was being finalized, I kept thinking to myself that this will be over soon, and then all the drama will stop, but it didn't. Over the years it has gotten a little bit better. I still have to stop my mom every time she talks about my dad, because I know that it will just turn into dad-bashing hour. It seems like every time I talk to my mother she has some new story about what my dad did this time, even 3 years later. I just tell her that she did not come to visit me at school to bitch about dad, and that while she's here we're not going to talk about it. I've come to the point where I know my dad well enough, that I know what not to expect and I don't need my mother constantly reminding me, now she just needs to realize that.

My mother has been my backbone throughout their separation, divorce, and aftermath. She needs someone to talk to and I'm that someone, and I listen, but sometimes enough is enough. She tries really hard to make up for all the times my dad has promised to be there and hasn't shown up, or all the plans he makes and then breaks, or all the phone calls I never get. She tries to make up for that, and I appreciate that, but she can't take my dad's place when he messes up, and she can't take away that pain. She's a great mom, and my dad could be a great dad, but I think I've come to real-ize that maybe my dad just wasn't meant to be a dad. Over the years, I have had many realizations about my father. I've forgiven him somewhat for leaving and not telling me, but I still have a long road ahead in forgiving him for not being a good father. My dad is a great person, and when we do spend time together we have a great time, but it's more like we're just friends, we don't have a father–daughter relationship. We still don't talk more than about once a month or once every 2 months, but that is progress for us. We used to never talk at all. After my freshman year at college things started to change. I became very upset that summer with my father and all of my hostility towards him finally came out, especially after I learned that he had no idea where I had been living or my phone number. I made him realize the importance of him being there for his children, and since then things have slowly changed. Even though the change is slow, it's a huge step in the right direction.

I know that the effects of my parents' divorce will not heal overnight, and it will take many years to get to a happy medium for everyone involved. My sister is now feeling the same feelings I felt when I was in high school, and my bother and I have come to an acceptance and are working on moving from there. When my brother and I finally come to terms, we will then have to help our little sister come with her own terms, the acceptance that we don't have a perfect family.

When Jasmine spoke to our class about her parents' divorce, it really hit home. I remember sitting in my seat shaking my head in agreement, just to say I know what you mean. Jasmine and I have different stories, but I can bet we probably share a few of the same feelings. I know she mentioned her feelings of abandonment from her mother, as did I with my father. I know that she felt like she had to be strong for her sister, as do I with my siblings. I still feel that I have to be strong for my siblings, but I've also come to realize that it's OK to not be strong all the time.

Comment

This woman's narrative reveals the picture of a hostile divorce that has not improved in time. It is obvious that the children in the family, including the respondent, are having a hard time coping because of the "mud-slinging" that has not ended since the divorce. This woman's pain also appears to be one of daily angst and feelings of loss, accompanied by vivid memories of what her family was like at one time and what then happened as the family came unwound. As she notes, her story is not that unusual in the accounts of children of divorce. It corresponds to ex-spouse interaction patterns that Ahrons (1994) referred to as *angry associates*. One can only hope that her parents will someday reach the more civil and redeeming category that Ahrons referred to as *cooperative colleagues,* as they work more collaboratively to address the needs of their children.

DIFFICULTY IN ACCEPTING A STEPFATHER

In the following account, a 21-year-old woman tells how she eventually learned to appreciate her new stepfather. Her account is typical of how difficult establishing new parental relationships may be for young people faced first with divorce and then with new, blended families.

I, like many other children today, grew up in a broken home. My mother and father were constantly fighting. I can remember waking up in the morning when I was in elementary school to the sound of dishes being put away while my parents fought. Although I can't remember any topics of the fights they had, it was a common occurrence and after my father slammed the door as he left, I went back to sleep. It was life to me and to tell the truth I don't remember thinking anything of it; that's the way parents are supposed to be. It seemed almost instantaneous when my parents separated. My common day to day life became my old life and I was thrown into a new one. The day I found out my parents were getting a divorce I was confused, at only 9 years old, not really realizing the severity of the situation. I don't remember how they told us but I do remember helping my dad pack up his things and voicing to everyone I loved that I had chosen to go with my father. In almost a blink of an eye I spent only weekends with my father and my mother was dating my principal (at my school).

Everything moved quickly after that. I don't remember a lot other than overall feelings I felt. My mother wanted my sister and I to embrace her new boyfriend and to love him like she did. I had conflicting thoughts all the time, I loved my mother and wanted to please her but I hated her boyfriend. The feelings obviously got too strong for even the people around me to handle because they had me transfer schools; therefore I wouldn't ruin my mother's lover's reputation.

I didn't understand how my sister was taking the situation so lightly. He was not my father, I didn't want him in my life and there was no way in hell he was going to replace my father, as I thought my mother intended. I began to throw temper-tantrums. I swore at my mother's boyfriend and announced my hatred to him every time he asked me to do anything or said anything I didn't like. By this time we had all moved into a house together and I continuously ran away to my father's apartment or called him frantic about a situation. At the time I didn't realize how much hurt I was causing everyone around me.

Then they began sending me to counseling. I went every Wednesday to talk about my feelings. The sessions didn't last very long because I didn't talk, out of spite mostly. I almost looked forward to the sessions because I felt I was showing them up and the fact that I got to eat Wendy's. During this time we went on a family vacation with my mom, her fiancé and my siblings. In the middle of the trip I made a huge scene at the resort that we were staying at in Wyoming and my mother decided to send me home.

My mother married my old principal and we all moved to Montana. I felt even further away from my father, not just physically but emotionally. I withdrew from my mother and new stepfather more and more. I became very independent and didn't want to accept anything from my new family. I still didn't take anything my stepfather said seriously, and didn't realize the knowledge that he encompassed.

It took me until my junior year in high school to get to the point that I could talk to my stepfather and actually take his advice to heart. Although I know that all of my insecurities were in my head I felt abandoned at the time, feeling that no one wanted to listen to me or cared about my feelings. I withdrew into myself even further, only causing myself more pain, but at the

*time I used it as a device mechanism. Now I am close with my stepfather,
and overall am glad that I went through everything that I did.*

Comment

This woman's account reveals some of the difficulties that new
stepfamilies have in achieving a sense of cohesiveness. She does
not discuss how she became close to her stepfather, but one can
read into her account the fact that this process was facilitated by
her new stepfamily having the financial assets to send her to counseling. That may be an essential step for many young people who
feel hurt and anger toward one or both of their parents and toward
the people with whom their parents are choosing to be romantically involved after divorce.

FINDING SANITY IN A CHAOTIC WORLD

Chaos and Craziness in the Postdivorce Family

This final story in this chapter, a 21-year-old woman shows a mind
that has countenanced much of the chaos and instability (including multiple divorces) that many students describe in their divorced families. Note her eloquence in describing how her father's
"heart dried up," like the oil fields on which he worked.

*I thought it was very brave of the guest panel to speak out about their ex-
perience of loss associated with divorce. I related well to most of what this
guest panel said. I have been very much affected and molded by divorce. My
parents divorced when I was 8 years old. Up to that point I would say I had
the typical all-American family. My father was a petroleum engineer and
my mother stayed at home with her three little girls. The oil fields soon dried
up and so did my father's heart. Little did I know that things were bad long
before I was told my father had been transferred from my birthplace to the
Western U.S. Dad went out a month or so before the rest of us. He was supposed to find and get our nice big "brand new" house ready. What he found
was a girlfriend (soon-to-be-wife) with her two kids of her own. My mom, sisters, and I didn't find that out until a few weeks after we moved out to the*

Western U.S. Then one morning before school, our parents were fighting. My older sister and I were in the living room where my mom was standing right in front of our father. My little sister was looking down from the loft when we heard the words that changed all of our lives forever, "Leave." Leave we did, as soon as he left for work. My mom loaded us girls up in the van and made the long journey to our home state in the Midwest and our grandparents' house, in silence the whole trip.

One of our guest speakers was also one of three sisters and her father also said he didn't love her mother anymore. I related to her story and remembered my own when she spoke. She stayed with her grandparents after her parents split too. We moved into an apartment nearby our grandparents. This apartment was small and crappy. My mother got on her feet and we moved into a nearby condominium. This was the fifth place I had lived in the last 2 months and fourth school. My dad didn't write, didn't call, didn't send birthday cards, and didn't come around again until he found out that my mom's new husband was taking us to Europe for the summer when I was 11. But I am jumping ahead.

My mom remarried a year after my father and her divorced. I hated my new stepdad. Not only was he mean but we were going to have to move from our condo in the West to Iowa. I did not want to leave my family and did not want to move to Iowa. So my father became a dad when he felt like it once every blue moon and I learned to adjust. My mother and stepfather fought all the time. Nowadays it's called being verbally abusive. The only good thing to come out of this marriage was the birth of my little brother. I love him so much. But again, this marriage ended in divorce. This divorce was not as difficult as the first. It actually was probably for the best. My ex-stepdad and I now get along. He's worked on his anger and I turn to him for fatherly advice.

I can also relate with the other guest speaker. She said her mom went out a lot and spent the child support money. To say my mom dated is an understatement! She got a lock on her bedroom door, her own phone line, and [a] personal ad. I don't think I would have had a problem with all that had she taken care of us, cooked, bought groceries, come home at night, or gone to any of my performances. I was on the pom-pom squad in high school. The summer after my junior year she met her "soul mate" Jim. He and my mom were married in Las Vegas after three months of dating. He was harmless but the whole situation was awkward. He moved in with us. My mom met her mother-in-law and most of his family after they were already married! My freshman year of college was laced with divorce. My older sister and her husband of four years divorced. My mom and Jim divorced. He lives nearby her house now. My little brother likes to spend time with him and my mom still asks him to do things around the house. Divorce has pretty much made its mark on my life thus far. I am sure I have not seen the last of it!

Comment

This final account continues a theme of complex family relations due in part to multiple divorces. Parents who read this account should take note of this young woman's description of her mother's dating life after the second divorce. The respondent did not object to a vibrant dating life for her mother. She did object, however, to what she felt was her mother's neglect of her and her siblings. This dilemma is played out in countless households. The newly single adult must figure out how to be a parent at the same time that she or he tries to develop and maintain new romantic relationships. The dilemma often is like the glass ball metaphor—there are rubber balls that can be dropped without harm, while there are glass balls that shatter when they drop. Parenting is a glass ball in this story and in all of the stories in this chapter in general.

CONCLUSIONS

The stories in this chapter speak to the centrality of the family, however complicated and constituted, in our lives. Families are by definition intricate and delicately operating entities. They often defy understanding under the best of conditions. They show both fragility and resilience. When in grave conflict and possible disintegration, families may be both enigmas and sources of abiding pain for their young members. There is no better support for any human than a strong, loving family. As Thomas Jefferson once said, "The happiest moments of my life have been the few which I have passed at home in the bosom of my family."

It is a tribute, then, that so many of the stories in this chapter have evolved from perceived chaos to the point at which the young person feels some hope and has found a course that makes sense for now. The constant in such stories is the fact of having to grow up and to do so early in life. Although these young people may have preferred to have grown up in tranquil, well-functioning families, they, like many of their peers did not have that luxury. Many of them still found ways to thrive in these tumultuous conditions.

We see in these stories many subcurrents of the American family in this century. There are multifaceted relationships in stepfamilies. There are ex-stepparents still playing key roles in children's growing up and adult life. There are angry, unresolved divorce-related feelings and patterns in many families, whereas there are more resolved, cooperative approaches being taken by still other families in which divorce has occurred.

These stories (e.g., the two long introductory narratives) are remarkable in showing complicated family patterns involving diverse parent figures (including stepparents), multiple stepsiblings, and the conclusion that "family" often has little to do with biological/legal ties (e.g., consider how the first respondent in this chapter now considers his ex-stepmother's family to be his closest family). Multiple divorce was a key factor in these complicated human chains of events. With a continuing high divorce rate for second and later marriages, one can only imagine the complex family relations that await many young people into the next century.

Just as noteworthy is these young persons' ability to be open and to express their feelings about their families and their difficulties with clarity and purpose. Many of these young people surely show what therapists have called *parentification*, or having to take on parental duties, such as working with siblings in parent-like roles. We worry about the long-term harm that may unfold as a consequence of these responsibilities. Also, though, we may be heartened by the courage and strength of mind shown by our respondents in these complex situations. They are obtaining college degrees, often have successful adult close relationships, and, most important, they appear to be knowledgeable about and open to the lifelong process ahead of them in dealing with their losses associated with divorce and family instability.

> *I am a "child of divorce." It's like saying I am an alcoholic, it's very hard.*
>
> —A woman whose story was told in this chapter

CHAPTER

7

CONCLUSIONS

In this final chapter, we draw conclusions about children's divorce experiences from their own narrative accounts written when they were college students. What have these articulate students' stories taught us about how divorce affected their lives? These narratives certainly do not provide any direct information regarding the students' level of adjustment, such as what would be provided had we administered tests of their levels of depression, their self-esteem, or their college academic performance. However, providing such objective information was not our intent in this project. Rather, consistent with our purpose to give voice to young adults who have experienced parental divorce, these stories provide a window into understanding young adults' *perceptions* of a variety of divorce-related phenomena, including divorce itself, how the divorce process unfolded for them, how divorce affected them in the short run, and how their subsequent lives were influenced by their parents' divorce.

Thanks to the opportunity provided by the students allowing us access to this window into their experience, this chapter contains three sections: a) an exploration of how some of the themes presented in chapter 1 were (or were not) illuminated by these students' narratives, b) a presentation of some additional themes that emerged from our analysis that extend beyond the extant literature, and c) some concluding comments regarding the importance of providing young people who have experienced parental divorce an opportunity to share their thoughts and feelings as their experience unfolds.

CONNECTIONS TO THE DIVORCE LITERATURE

Back to Emery's (1999) Conclusions

As we described in chapter 1, Emery (1999) offered a set of balanced conclusions about the impact of divorce on children. Each of his conclusions has been found to have merit in the narratives reported in this book. Emery's first "fact" was that divorce causes a great deal of stress for children. Consistent with this point, young people reported that stress was a frequent concomitant of the divorce in their families, before, during, and after the actual divorce. Emery's second fact was that divorce increases the risk of psychological problems. Although we did not administer any measures that would allow us to specifically determine whether our participants had any clinically significant psychological problems, there was frequent mention of varied intrapersonal (e.g., depression, anxiety, sense of being different) and interpersonal problems (e.g., distrust of romantic partners, pessimistic view of marriage, turbulent relationship experiences). A minority of the participants in our project clearly *felt* that they had experienced psychological problems, typically in the short term.

Emery's (1999) third fact was that most children of divorced parents function as well as children from first-marriage families. The narratives of these young people, even sometimes including those who reported that they had had psychological problems, suggest a high level of functioning, comparable to that of children from families that are both intact and happy. Of course, the fact that all of our respondents were enrolled in college suggests that they are both reasonably well functioning and potentially not representative of the larger population of young adults whose parents have divorced. Emery's fourth fact is that children whose parents divorce report considerable pain, unhappy memories, and continued distress. It is clear that some of our respondents provided narratives containing painful and unpleasant memories, as well as a continued sense of distress.

Emery's (1999) fifth and final fact is that there are considerable individual differences in children's adjustment after divorce, and these differences are influenced by aspects of postdivorce family life. Emery's suggestion that individual differences are common is well illustrated throughout the narratives. These narratives show a wide spectrum of empathy, maturity, civility, and responsible action, both on the part of parents and of their children. Furthermore, the accounts presented in this book show the influential nature of postdivorce family processes, including the extent to which the parents place their children in the middle of their conflicts, the extent of involvement by the nonresidential parent, the potential involvement of new adults (e.g., stepparents) in the children's lives, the quality of the relationship between the children and the residential parent, the financial standing of the family, the extent to which the siblings in the family depend on one another, the extent to which the children are placed in the role of adult to assist a parent who is depressed or acting out, and whether the postdivorce family members live in close geographical proximity. Given these and many other factors too numerous to name, one may conclude that "it depends" remains a key phrase in describing the experiences of children of divorce—particularly in regard to postdivorce adjustment, which depends on a variety of pre- and postdivorce family factors.

"What About the Kids?"

This section title reflects the title of a recent book by Wallerstein and Blakeslee (2003) in which they make a set of strong recommendations to parents who are divorcing and who want to help their children get through the experience with minimal psychological damage. One of the most compelling points they make is that when parents fight bitterly, the children's sense of loss, grief—and, sometimes, terror—is boundless. We have witnessed examples of these feelings in the present book. Wallerstein and

Blakeslee made the cogent point that parents in caretaking roles have an obligation to accord respect even to the parent who may be "absent in action." As they say, a good input to the children in a divorcing family may go something like: "You are all wonderful children and I am so proud of you. If Daddy were here, he would be proud of you, too" (p. 83).

Another important idea conveyed by Wallerstein and Blakeslee (2003) is that divorcing parents need to be especially sensitive not to overburden the children. Our respondents too often mentioned their hurt and despair at being placed in the middle between warring ex-spouses. Parents need to have perspective about their children's own developmental needs during this difficult time. They need to be aware of so-called "parentification" tendencies on their part (i.e., the tendency to treat their older children like partners or "little parent figures"). Many children will want to help and are adroit in their already-developed skills as well as their love for their parents and their desire to be there for hurting adults. Nevertheless, parents need to protect them from getting too involved and taking on too many duties (including that of an informal therapist).

In short, parents need to keep some distance between themselves and their relationship dilemmas and their children, who have their own needs and agendas. As we have seen repeatedly in the narratives, children may learn a great deal about people and life, and they mature well beyond their years during these periods of family disruption. Still, they do not need to take on undue burdens of parent-like responsibilities when they face their own hurdles in developing close relationships, academic learning, learning about the work world, physical fitness training, and the like.

A powerful conclusion of Wallerstein and Blakeslee's (2003) analysis emphasizes the role of modeling responsibility, sensitivity, and empathy on the part of parents in the divorce experience:

> During and after your divorce, your children will observe you carefully. They're looking to you for guidance because they've been shaken by the divorce and are worried that love is fleeting and close relationships are fragile or even doomed to fail. They look to you for clues to guide their own lives and for encouragement that love can be strong and lasting. They need to believe that parents

are faithful forever in caring for their children ... Human beings
who have hurt each other can forgive and go on to treat each other
with civility. (p. 364)

"Good Enough Marriage" or "Good Enough Divorce"

One of the most controversial of Wallerstein et al.'s (2000b) claims is that a "good enough marriage" without violence, martyrdom, or severe mental disorder will be satisfactory for children. They argued that children from such "good enough marriages" will adjust better in their own adult interpersonal relationships than will children from even happily divorced families. The narratives presented in this book cannot conclusively answer this question, partly because we did not sample narratives from college students whose parents were still married. Nevertheless, several participants commented on Wallerstein et al.'s (2000b) claim, and those who did consistently disagreed with the "good-enough marriage" notion. As a group, their primary reason for disagreeing with Wallerstein et al. (2000b) was that the divorce, although perhaps quite painful and disruptive in the short run, allowed for a more growth-producing environment in which to be raised, with less conflict and more cohesive and secure family relationships.

By contrast, Constance Ahrons (1994) argued that some divorces can be managed in a healthy manner that serves the children well in the long run. This notion of the "good divorce" was reinforced by the narratives in this book. At the time of divorce, parents who worked hard to be civil and sensitive to family needs are setting the stage for a much smoother long-term ride for their children, as the children assimilate the meanings of the divorce and adjust their lives to the new contingencies. In her studies, Ahrons points to a relatively large percentage of ex-couples who show behavior reflective of "cooperative colleagues," which is a category that tends to facilitate the adjustment of the children. This type of ex-partner arrangement shows a general orientation of collaboration between parents, as shown in Table 7.1.

Ahrons's (1994) thesis about the good divorce sometimes has been criticized as suggesting that divorce is normal—maybe even serving as an encouragement of divorce. We believe that her thesis importantly recognizes the facts of life involved with not only a

TABLE 7.1
Characteristics of Ahrons's (1994) "Cooperative Colleagues"

- The ex-partners work well together on issues dealing with children.
- They usually can compromise when dealing with division of holidays and other major challenges of coparenting, including visitation and provision for the children's needs.
- They usually spend some special occasions together as a "binuclear family," at events such as plays and athletic events, school graduation, and weddings.
- They are able to separate issues surrounding the former marital relationship from issues surrounding the long-term parenting obligations

high divorce rate in the past but also, by all indications, a continuing high divorce rate well into the future. If divorce has to happen, we as a society have to learn how to manage it so that fewer people are devastated by its consequences. A final set of Ahrons's recommendations to parents coheres well with the thrust of commentaries by young people in this book:

> *Slow down the process—children need time to adjust. Accept that your child needs—and has a right to—both parents. Cooperate with your ex if only for the sake of the children. Establish a limited partnership agreement with clear rules. Accept that your child's family will expand to include nonbiological kin. (p. 252)*

We fully agree with this advice. It is an act of tremendous graciousness to allow—even help—one's child love her or his other parent, especially one who has been very hurtful. Yet it is an act that many people can do, and parents will later learn how powerfully constructive it was in the child's adjustment. Indeed, we applaud Ahrons's (1994) unique ideas and do not believe that she is promoting divorce by taking this realistic view of it.

Hetherington's "For Better or For Worse"

On the basis of three longitudinal, large-sample studies of children and families, Hetherington and Kelly (2002) drew conclusions that are quite similar to those Emery (1999) drew: Divorce can have devastating and painful effects, but most children cope quite well in the long term, and divorce can even have considerable "positive effects" (Hetherington & Kelly, 2002, p. 5). These positive effects can be preventative in nature (e.g., enabling children and adults to escape violent and unsafe home environments), but they also can provide opportunities for "life-transforming personal growth," particularly for girls and women. Hetherington and Kelly also called attention to the "divorce revolution" that has led to a much wider range of life choices and options and, hence, to greater complexity and diversity in family life than was true 40 years ago. Because of this diversity, as noted in chapter 1, Hetherington and Kelly argued that statements such as "Divorce is harmful to children" and "Divorce has major long-term negative effects" are overly simplistic and unlikely to generalize to the majority of people who experience divorce, because they do not take into account a host of contextual variables that affect divorce adjustment.

The narratives presented in this book were very consistent with many of Hetherington and Kelly's (2002) claims. The recurring themes of pain and loss were certainly evident throughout the participants' narrative accounts, and we do not wish to minimize the impacts that these negative emotions can and do have on children of divorce. However, several participants also wrote eloquently about the opportunities that they felt became available to them because of the divorce and divorce-related changes. These opportunities were provided to them because of a variety of factors, such as being able to observe a healthy and well-functioning romantic relationship after one of their parents remarried, having additional financial resources with the addition of a stepparent into the household, being given responsibilities that they would not otherwise have had (e.g., supervising younger siblings), becoming part of a more stable postdivorce family unit, and benefiting from having new siblings with whom they could interact with and in whom they could sometimes confide. The narratives also vividly showed the complexity and diversity of modern-day family life to which Hetherington and Kelly (2002) referred to. Even in a sample that is likely to be more homogeneous (i.e., college students from the Midwest) than the larger population of children of divorce, the stories revealed both considerable variation in household and family structure (e.g., who is living in the household and who is considered to be a member of the family) and frequent transitions (e.g., geographic moves, the addition of or removal of individuals living in the household, the remarriage and/or subsequent divorce of one or both parents). Our sense is that the participants in our project would consider many of Hetherington and Kelly's conclusions to resonate well with their own experience.

Stahl's "The Love They Lost"

As discussed in chapter 1, Stahl (2000) found, on the basis of interviews, that young people felt a sense of a void in their lives, partly stemming from not having access to a successful model of a well-functioning couple. She also found that her respondents had a variety of other negative life experiences (see Table 1.2), including a fear of feeling (i.e., numbness); a fear of abandonment by loved ones; negative emotions resulting from the violation of the children's expectations of family; a sense that they were not allowed to experience a normal childhood; uncertainty about romantic decisions; patterns of acting out against authority; and difficulty relating to both parents, particularly a parent who may have been absent (or uninvolved) during the person's formative years. On the more positive side, Stahl's respondents seemed to mature relatively early in life and, among those who themselves divorced as adults, they felt that they were able to manage the divorce process in a way that was respectful of their children's needs and feelings—in a way that they perhaps had felt that their own parents had not done for them.

Our respondents' narratives speak in some interesting ways to the themes identified from Stahl's (2000) interviews. On the one hand, many of the respondents in our project—particularly those represented in chapters 3, 5, and 6—echoed some of the same negative themes found in Table 1.2 as well as some of the positive ones, particularly among those whose narratives are re-ported in chapter 4. However, our respondents also made some claims that seem a bit discrepant from those of Stahl. In particu-lar, a number of our participants felt that they had been exposed to positive romantic relationship role models after one (or both) of their parents remarried following divorce. We saw numerous instances of situations when the stepparent became the "real" parent to the child and one clear instance in which the steppar-ent became the primary adult caretaker of the young adult and the foundation of what this individual now considered to be his family. Although there has been a considerable body of research on the effects on children of living in a stepfamily (see Coleman, Ganong, & Fine, 2000), just as in the case of the divorce experi-ence, we know little about how young adults themselves construe their experiences living with a stepparent. More research is clearly needed into this area.

"A Generation at Risk"

Amato and Booth (1997) explored issues that have created consid-erable upheaval under the title of "a generation at risk." Do our narratives help address this risk issue? We argue that, to some de-gree, they do. They suggest that amidst the pain of young people who have suffered from divorce and continuing instability in their parents' close relationships, and their families in general, there of-ten is a lot of learning going on. Some strong individuals appear to be emerging. Along these lines, we would like to emphasize the positive growth found particularly in the stories in chapter 4.

Surely, there are many who show great hurt and who are cynical about romantic closeness. But even the most cynical of these sto-ries often showed thoughtful reflection, humor, and grace in com-menting on painful events in their families. Thus, overall, there is clearly considerable risk associated with being young and being in a time of restlessness in our closest relationships, but it is unclear how much of this additional risk stems from the divorce experi-ence itself or from its associated characteristics, such as parental conflict, low-quality parent–child relationships, and/or a lack of supervision of children. The instability in these young adults' lives will not likely change anytime soon; however, we can be reassured by our respondents' hope and resolve to make strong bonds with their own romantic partners and future nuclear families.

Resiliency

A major theme in this book is the resiliency of many children of divorce. They have assimilated the divorce as best they can and have used the energy it conveyed in positive ways in their thinking, feelings, and behavior. The career work of Hollywood film director Steven Spielberg is illustrative of this use of divorce-loss energy in a positive way. Spielberg indicates that he has learned from his parents' divorce, as well as from his own divorce, and that some of those lessons have found their way into how he makes films and the contributions he hopes these films make. Spielberg says that his parents' divorce is a subject that is "woven into him" and that he will continue making movies that relate to the divorce. In commenting on a recently directed film "Catch Me If You Can," Spielberg had this to say about his parents' divorce:

> *Certainly you have to be happy in your life ... I wish my parents had divorced five years before they did because they weren't happy for five years, and we were more miserable living with that. Had it been a clean break, we wouldn't have had to have five years of hearing the fighting coming through the heating vents from their bedroom to ours and hearing all the yelling. I'm as happy as I've ever been. Kate Capshaw is my partner, my wife, and I've got a great family. (Caro, 2002, p. MW6)*

EXTENSIONS OF THE EXISTING LITERATURE: NEWLY EMERGING THEMES

In this section we elaborate on two themes that emerged strongly from the participants' stories: (a) that divorce is associated with considerable pain that may take different forms, at different times, after the divorce, and (b) that it is important to recognize that the construct of grieving very aptly characterizes what most young people experience. Although these themes have been mentioned to some degree earlier in this book and have been noted in some form by some divorce scholars, they have received relatively less attention in the literature than the themes noted in the preceding section.

A Painful Tune

Overall, divorce is painful even for the young people who echoed Spielberg's point that, in his family, the divorce was best for all (Caro, 2002). The tenor of pain and despair is clearly seen in many of the narratives of this book. For so many, expectations have been dashed. These expectations pertain to the "perfect family," or what to expect in the daily life of a family, or what to expect from parents in the big events of a young person's life (graduation, athletic contests, weddings, birth of children, etc.). New expectations have to be developed. New "players," including dating partners brought in by parents, new stepparents, and stepsiblings, come onto the child's stage of development. The degree of cognitive framing and assimilation for many children in these changing family circumstances is enormous.

It is interesting, however, that even in the bleakest of divorce fights and the most chaotic of families, children survived. That is a principal idea in Emery's (1999) analysis. This counter to the pain tenor is highlighted by the fact that our respondents are moving along in their college careers. They often are flourishing in their interpersonal lives as well. Although the degree of success appears to vary for these areas of accomplishment, this set of respondents showed an overall resiliency and unwillingness to submit to hopelessness and helplessness. Furthermore, some of the most scarred young people reported a resolve to develop their own interpersonal lives and families in ways that avoided some of the most egregious aspects of marriage and family life that they had observed in their families.

A common pragmatic expression that symbolizes the reality orientation of many young people coping with their parents' divorce is "It's just what it is." That recognition applies to their own family situation and to the omnipresent nature of divorce in the lives of people around them. They seem to recognize that perfection is far from the normal state of affairs in dating and mating. However, such recognition does not suggest a lack of feeling about their loss or a diminished passion to have a relationship of their own that does not lead to divorce.

A Lot About Grieving

The narratives in this book have had a clear emphasis on grieving and coping with grief. Many of these narratives were collected in a course titled "Loss and Trauma" (Harvey & Hofman, 2002). Thus, it is entirely possible that the respondents were highly self-selected in that they were interested in exploring and writing about the loss aspects of their parents' divorce and their ongoing feelings about the divorce. At the same time, it is interesting to note that many students taking this course have said that, before studying the topic of children of divorce, they did not consider their parents' divorce to involve much of a loss for them; neither did they feel the need to grieve. Although, we might hope that this benign state of affairs would continue in these students' minds, unfortunately for many it does not. Even quite civil divorces usually involve considerable loss. In time, that fact becomes evident, as does the urge to grieve. It may be the case that such students in this class gain this latter perspective more quickly in their young adult lives.

In studying the losses associated with parental divorce, many young people learn that they own their pain and have every right to express it. They also learn that they have the right to know more about the "whys" of their parents' divorce. More generally, though, they learn to place this loss within the context of other losses that people experience. Life is filled with a broad spectrum of loss, from death and divorce, to illness and injury, to being the target of discrimination and humiliation. Somewhere within that array, which may occur to disproportionate degrees in any one person's life, children of divorce locate themselves and their parents. We hope they learn to value the lessons of loss that may accrue from most losses people experience.

In the "Loss and Trauma" course, students read Viktor Frankl's (1959) *Man's Search for Meaning*. This memoir tells of Frankl's experiences and losses in Nazi death camps. It is a resoundingly positive work in which Frankl uses his losses to give back to others in the form of his theory of logotherapy and his profound philosophy of hope and the will to survive.

Being a child of divorce sometimes has much in common with being a survivor of great trauma (Garbarino, 1995). As Frankl (1959) suggested, each of us is searching for ways to make our lives more meaningful. For some, the search is more daunting than it is for others. The same is true for children of divorce who are attempting to understand their parents' divorce and their own reactions to it. Many seem to rise nobly to the challenge. Others seem to be broken by it. A lesson found in studying major loss is that one's coping is a lifelong task (Harvey, 2001; Harvey & Miller, 1998). We often will have to cope with huge pileups of loss. Many young people have begun to learn these lessons of loss quite early. We hope they will learn to appreciate the Frankl-like spirit of survival and finding meaning in these situations.

As some of the narratives noted, young people's sense of loss and grief associated with their parents' divorce paralleled the idea of *disenfranchised loss and grief* (see Doka, 2002). Such losses are not well recognized or supported in society; thus, the need to grieve likewise is not well recognized or supported. Children of divorce often feel that people (even their parents) do not appreciate the depth of their feelings of loss and their need to grieve. After all, divorce is common. Many parents may believe that they have done a good job in immunizing their children against the sense of major loss and the need to grieve; however, one cannot totally immunize people against such a violation of what they believe and hope will transpire in their lives (Janoff-Bulman, 1992). Furthermore, most of us feel the need to grieve major losses. Our respondents probably were more attuned to this need than are many other people. They wrote about their feelings of loss at a relatively early age. Such a step bodes well for their long-term adjustment to their parents' divorce and its many lasting consequences.

FINAL CONCLUSION: MANY SHADES OF TRUTH AND THE NEED TO TALK AND EXPRESS THOUGHTS AND FEELINGS

A pervasive theme of the narratives in this book is that there are no monolithic truths that characterize the experiences of children of divorce; rather, there are many truths, and these shades of truth are quite likely to ebb and flow over time. There are many types of experience, from dismal to quite positive and uplifting, to many in-betweens. For some children of divorce, their sense of loss based on the divorce is so removed from their daily lives that they may report that there have been no major consequences associated with their parents' divorce. For other children of divorce, the sense of loss is current and palpable. They sometimes express the feeling that there is no relief in sight from their painful thoughts and experiences.

Our glimpse at the lives of children of divorce was limited by the fact that the narratives were presented at only one point in time and pertain to different periods of time and experience for different respondents. As we noted in chapter 1, changes in how children perceive their parents' divorce are likely as the children develop and experience their own relationships and the loss of such relationships. Some young people showed in these narratives that their perspective is becoming clearer over time. Almost all of them now have experienced their own relationship difficulties. They now are less naïve about the struggles to make some relationships work. They see better the subtleties of thought and feeling that go into long-term relating. In short, they already are becoming sophisticated relationship theorists in their own right and translating some of their understanding into their ideas about their family and parents' experiences of love and loss. On the basis of the narratives, one sees that critical to this development is an openness between parents and children about the marriage and general problems the parents are facing in relating well over time. To the extent that young people can openly discuss positions about what happened and why it happened, it appears that the young people grow in understanding of the diversity of behavior often displayed in these circumstances.

For other children of divorce, their perspective remains obfuscated by too many unknowns and too much avoidance of discussing the issues by parents. There often is a theory at work that if one does not talk about it, the pain will be lessened more quickly. That stance obviously does not comport well with many of the narratives reported in this book. As many young people cried out for in their reports, talk about the divorce and its implications is essential. Parents have an obligation to recognize children's interest in their stories and the stories of their ex-partners as well as their need to express their feelings of loss as children involved in these situations.

An overriding conclusion of this collection of narratives is that young people in their teens and 20s greatly desire a forum in which they can express their thoughts and feelings about their parents' divorce and divorce in general. They frequently reported limited opportunities to discuss their experiences. They also reported that significant people in their lives—from parents, to teachers, to coaches, to clergy—have not promoted dialogue about these experiences. Furthermore, even their peers may be closed off to discussions. Only people who have had similar experiences may be more willing to probe the topic.

Young people want a voice about divorce. To have such a voice is to empower oneself to analyze and learn, to share and confide. To have a voice is to be able to learn, show empathy, and be helpful to others who also have felt the pain of divorce. Telling one's story, as Coles (1989) eloquently argued, is our bedrock capacity as humans, and being allowed and able to confide about our biggest losses is one our most humanizing acts. We have seen in this book that this capacity to confide about issues and be open to one's losses is critical both for the child and the parent in the divorcing situation.

REFERENCES

Ahrons, C. (1994). *The good divorce.* New York: HarperCollins.

Amato, P. (2000). The consequences of divorce for adults and children. *Journal of Marriage and the Family, 62,* 1269–1287.

Amato, P., & Booth, A. (1997). *A generation at risk: Growing up in an era of family upheaval.* Cambridge, MA: Harvard University Press.

Amato, P. R., & DeBoer, D. D. (2001). The transmission of marital instability across generations: Relationship skills or commitment to marriage. *Journal of Marriage and the Family, 63,* 1038–1051.

Amato, P., & Keith, B. (1991). Parental divorce and the well-being of children: A meta-analysis. *Psychological Bulletin, 110,* 26–46.

Blankenhorn, D. (1995). *Fatherless America.* New York: Basic Books.

Bochner, A. P., Ellis, C., & Tillmann-Healy, L. M. (1997). Relationships as stories. In S. Duck (Ed.), *Handbook of personal relationships* (2nd ed., pp. 307–324). Chichester, England: Wiley.

Bogenschneider, K. (2000). Has family policy come of age? A decade review of the state of U.S. family policy in the 1990s. *Journal of Marriage and the Family, 62,* 1136–1159.

Booth, P., & Amato, P. (2001). Parental predivorce relations and offspring postdivorce well-being. *Journal of Marriage and the Family, 63,* 197–212.

Braver, S. (1998). *Divorced dads: Shattering the myths.* New York: Tarcher.

Braver, S. (2001, January 14). "The legacy of divorce?" *Dallas News,* p. 501.

Caro, M. (2002, December 26). Interview with Steven Spielberg. *Chicago Tribune*, p. MW6.

Carver, R. (1989). *What we talk about when we talk about love.* New York: Vintage.

Coleman, M., & Ganong, L. (1997). Stepfamilies from the stepfamily's perspective. *Marriage and Family Review, 26,* 107–121.

Coleman, M., Ganong, L., & Fine, M. (2000). Reinvestigating remarriage: Another decade of progress. *Journal of Marriage and the Family, 62,* 1288–1307.

Coleman, M., Ganong, L., & Weaver, S. (2001). families. In J. H. Harvey & A. Wenzel (Eds.), *Close romantic relationships: Maintenance and enhancement* (pp. 255–276). Mahwah, NJ: Lawrence Erlbaum Associates.

Coles, R. (1989). *The call of stories.* Boston: Houghton Mifflin.

Doka, K. J. (Ed.). (2002). *Disenfranchised grief: New directions, challenges and strategies for practice.* Champaign, IL: Research Press.

Egeland, B., Carlson, E., & Stroufe, L. A. (1993). Resilience as process. *Development and Psychopathology, 5,* 517–528.

Ellis, C. (1995). *Final negotiations.* Philadelphia: Temple University Press.

Emery, R. E. (1999). *Marriage, divorce, and children's adjustment.* Thousand Oaks, CA: Sage.

Feng, P., & Fine, M. A. (2000). Evaluation of a research-based parenting education program for divorcing parents: The Focus on Kids program. *Journal of Divorce and Remarriage, 34,* 1–23.

Feng, D., Giarrusso, R., Bengston, V. L., & Frye, N. (1999). Intergenerational transmission of marital quality and marital instability. *Journal of Marriage and the Family, 61,* 451–463.

Fine, M. A. (2000). Divorce and single parenting. In C. Hendrick & S. S. Hendrick (Eds.), *Sourcebook of close relationships* (pp. 139–152). Newbury Park, CA: Sage.

Fine, M. A., Coleman, M., Gable, S., Ganong, L. H., Ispa, J., Morrison, J., & Thornburg, K. R. (1999). Research-based parenting education for divorcing parents: A university–community collaboration. In T. R. Chibocos & R. M. Lerner (Eds.), *Serving children and families through community–university partnerships: Success stories* (pp. 249–256). Norwell, MA: Kluwer.

Fine, M. A., & Demo, D. H. (2000). Divorce: Societal ill or normative transition? R. M. Milardo & S. W. Duck (Eds.), *Families as relationships* (pp. 135–156). Chichester, England: Wiley.

Frankl, V. (1959). *Man's search for meaning.* New York: Washington Square Press.

Furstenberg, F. F., & Cherlin, A. (1991). *Divided families.* Newbury Park, CA: Sage.

Furstenberg, F. F., & Spanier, G. B. (1987). Remarriage and reconstituted families. In M. B. Sussman & S. K. Steinmetz (Eds.), *Handbook of marriage and the family* (pp. 419–434). New York: Plenum.

Furstenberg, F. F., & Teitler, J. O. (1994). Reconsidering the effects of marital disruption: What happens to children of divorce in early childhood? *Journal of Family Psychology, 11*, 489–502.

Garbarino, J. (1995). Growing up in a socially toxic environment: Life for children and families in the 1990s. In G. Melton (Ed.), *Nebraska Symposium on Motivation* (Vol. 42, pp. 1–20). Lincoln: University of Nebraska Press.

Gately, D., & Schwebel, A. I. (1992). Favorable outcomes in children after parental divorce. *Journal of Divorce and Remarriage, 18*, 57–63.

Harvey, J. H. (1996). *Embracing their memory: Loss and the social psychology of story-telling.* Needham Heights, MA: Allyn & Bacon.

Harvey, J. H. (2002). *Perspectives on loss and trauma.* Thousand Oaks, CA: Sage.

Harvey, J. H. (2001). The psychology of loss as a lens to a positive psychology. *American Behavioral Scientist, 44*, 838–853.

Harvey, J. H., & Hofmann, W. J. (2002). Teaching about loss: A special opportunity for psychology. *Teaching of Psychology, 29*, 319–320.

Harvey, J. H., & Miller, E. (1998). Toward a psychology of loss. *Psychological Science, 9*, 429–434.

Harvey, J. H., Weber, A. L., & Orbuch, T. L. (1990). *Interpersonal accounts: A social psychological perspective.* Oxford, England: Blackwell.

Hawkins, A. J., Nock, S. L., Wilson, J. C., Sanchez, L., & Wright, J. D. (2002). Attitudes toward covenant marriage and divorce: Policy implications from a three-state comparison. *Family Relations, 51*, 166–175.

Hetherington, E. M., & Kelly, J. (2002). *For better or for worse: Divorce reconsidered.* New York: Norton.

Janoff-Bulman, R. (1992). *Shattered assumptions.* New York: Free Press.

Lansford, J. E., Ceballo, R., Abbey, A., & Stewart, A. (2001) Does family structure matter? *Journal of Marriage and the Family, 63*, 840–851.

Levine, A. (2000). Helping your children cope with divorce at Christmas time. *Chicago Tribune,* C2.

Luthar, S. S. (1991). Vulnerability and resilience: A study of high-risk adolescents. *Child Development, 62*, 600–612.

McLanahan, S. S. (1999). Father absence and the welfare of children. In E. M. Hetherington (Ed.), *Coping with divorce, single parenting, and remarriage: A risk and resilience perspective* (pp. 117–145). Mahwah, NJ: Lawrence Erlbaum Associates.

Orbuch, T. L. (1997). People's accounts count: The sociology of accounts. *Annual Review of Sociology, 23*, 455–478.

Paul, P. (2002). *The starter marriage and the future of matrimony.* New York: Villard.

Pollitt, K. (2000, September 25). Is divorce getting a bum rap? *Time,* 82.

Snyder, C. R., & Lopez, S. J. (Eds.). (2002). *Handbook of positive psychology.* New York: Oxford University Press.

Stahl, S. (2000). *The love they lost.* New York: Delacorte Press.

U.S. Bureau of the Census. (2000, September 26). *Report on American families.* News release.

Wallerstein, J. S., & Blakeslee, S. (2003). *What about the kids?* New York: Hyperion.

Wallerstein, J. S., & Kelly, J. B. (1980). *Surviving the breakup.* New York: Basic Books.

Wallerstein, J. S., & Lewis, J. (1998). The long-term impact of divorce on children: A first report from a 25-year study. *Family & Conciliation Courts Review. 36,* 368–383.

Wallerstein, J. S., Lewis, J. M., & Blakeslee, S. (2000a, September 25). Fear of falling. *Time,* 85.

Wallerstein, J. S., Lewis, J. M., & Blakeslee, S. (2000b). *The unexpected legacy of divorce: A 25-year landmark study.* New York: Hyperion.

Weiss, R. S. (1975). *Marital separation.* New York: Basic Books.

Whitehead, B. D. (1996). *The divorce culture.* New York: Vintage.

Index